The Non-League Fo

Liverpool & I

by Terry Gorman

Photography by Terry Gorman, except where indicated

Series Editor: Mike Floate Series Consultant: Colin Peel

A Football Grounds Frenzy production.
Published by Newlands Photographic, 71 Stones Cross Road,
Crockenhill, Swanley, Kent BR8 8LT

Photo above: The stand and enclosure during a one-minutes silence at National Park in the interwar years. All of the men bar one have removed their hats and caps.

Front Cover (clockwise from left): Formby, Marine, Ashton United, Mossley. Back cover (clockwise from top): Bootle, Chadderton, Radcliffe Borough, Ramsbottom United, South Liverpool, Oldham Town.

ISBN 978-1-900257-22-0
Printed and bound by Catford Print, 3 Bellingham Rd London SE6 2PN
020 8695 0101 http://www.catfordprint.co.uk

Introduction

Originally I aimed to cover the whole of Lancashire, but there was too much material to do justice to some of the most interesting grounds in one book. Consequently I decided to split into two volumes – Liverpool and Manchester, and the rest of the county (published in 2009). Then I had to decide which ground slotted into which.

One league secretary suggested that I use affiliation to County FA as the guide, as the whole county is covered by the Lancashire, the Manchester and the Liverpool County Associations. However, this gave a different set of problems, as I found when reading the English FA`s "Memorandum on Areas and Overlapping of Associations", dated 25th August 1950 and 12th January 1951 – which refers to the "Overlapping Reports of 1908 and 1927".

If that is complicated, take some examples - Liverpool Ramblers are one of the oldest clubs in the city, but are members of the Lancashire FA. Barnoldswick Town play in the West Lancashire League, but are members of the West Riding of Yorkshire FA. To compound things, many clubs have multiple affiliations.

In the end the obvious grounds decided themselves, history and tradition provided guidelines, and I included the Liverpool County Premier League and the Manchester League, even though some clubs are outside Liverpool and Manchester, and excluded the West Lancashire League, even though some of its clubs are inside.

Current grounds (p4 - 55)

The two cities covered have an excellent range of quality grounds, homes to some well-known non-League clubs. I have included them in some sort of order of merit, with good old-fashioned venues cared for by dedicated volunteers given due credit for thoughtful maintenance.

Whilst appreciating the grading pressures which mean that many clubs resort to prefabricated seating units it is a shame that they remove much of the unique local character at the grounds which install them.

The Manchester League (p 56 - 65)

The Manchester League was formed in 1893, and has continued since then with a break only for WWI. In season 2007/8 there were 19 teams in the Premier Division, of which two – Wigan Robin Park and Irlam - have been elevated to the North West Counties Football Leage (NWCFL) for season 2008/9. Stockport Georgians, one of the remaining 17, featured in the Cheshire volume in this series and AFC Blackley folded.

Grounds are of a higher standard in terms of facilities when compared to the equivalent Liverpool League. Of the sixteen featured, seven have their own separate pitch and changing rooms, four share facilities with a cricket club, two ground-share, one pays £11,000 per annum to use Manchester City Academy`s 3rd generation artificial surface, and two others now play on artificial pitches. Three of the clubs which share a playing surface with cricket have overlapping pitches, which makes for some fascinating challenges.

We have also included four clubs from outside the 2008/9 Premier Division as they each have features of particular interest.

Liverpool County Premier League (p66-9)

Created in 2006 by the merger of the I Zingari Football League (founded in 1895) and the Liverpool County Combination (1908), this new Step 7 league was part of the FA restructuring of the national football scene. Of the sixteen clubs playing in the Premier Division in season 2007/8, five played on school or college pitches (one now sharing with Alder FC), five on public pitches, one was ground sharing, and five had their own pitch. One of these latter five was Ford Motors – unusual in having a stand, but as they play in Widnes their ground was included in the Cheshire volume of this series. In addition St Dominics F.C. have now folded. The Liverpool Ramblers entry is on page 65 but they are not members of this or any league.

Lost Grounds (p70 - 87)

The problem with this section was what to leave out, not find grounds to include. Two themes of de-industrialisation and increasing land prices mean that many grounds have disappeared.

Frank Hannah, the President of the Manchester FA, was himself involved for many years with Chloride Recreation, whose team featured in the FA Vase in the mid-1970s, but whose facilities now lie abandoned. He describes how the pitches in the Manchester Industrial League were amongst the best non-league grounds in the country. Similarly the Liverpool Business Houses League had some extremely high-quality facilities. To read the names in the tables from those two Leagues is like reading a roll of honour for our industrial past. Frank kindly gave me a list of grounds that had gone which in itself would have justified a complete book.

In the 1990s Bolton Metropolitan Borough Council commissioned university lecturer Peter Swain to prepare a report on amateur football within the Borough, with a focus on the facilities available. Peter recalls that he listed about 70 pitches that had disappeared in Bolton alone since the end of WWII – including the Bromwich Street pitches on which the Brazilians trained during the 1966 World Cup. He believes that the Council 'buried' the report.

The grounds in this section represent but a sample of those that have disappeared.

Acknowledgements

I have to begin by thanking my wife for her tolerance whilst I've been working on this, and my son for accompanying me on many of the trips (and my daughter-in-law for letting him.).

Club officials with whom I spoke were unfailingly helpful, and I would like to thank them for the information they gave. Sadly space doesn't permit me to name everyone who helped, but I would really like to mention those who didn't simply give information, but went to much more trouble than I had the right to expect:

Frank Hannah (Manchester FA), Alan Alcock (Northern Premier League), Rob Hurst and Ian Templeman (NWCFL), David Hills-Taylor & Jez Sayle (Ashton Utd), Kylie Wilcock (Atherton LR), Tony Onslow (who wrote "The Forgotten Rivals" about the original Bootle FC), Roy Haslam (Breightmet Utd), Jim Picken (Castleton Gabriels/Rochdale Town), David Greaves (Chadderton T), Graham Shuttleworth (Curzon Ashton), Robert Naylor (Daisy Hill), Alan Slater & David Siddall (Droylsden and the website, "Let there be Light"), Dave Dickinson (Formby), John Grundy (Hindsford), Warren Dodd (Irlam), John Mannion (Lucas Sports), Ron Young (Maghull), David Wotherspoon (Marine & author of "The Mighty Mariners"), John Cawthorne (Mossley), David Shepherd (Oldham T), Ben Mallett (Old Xaverians), Kevin Horry, Denis Bellairs (Prescot Cables), Alan Michaelovitz (Prestwich Heys), Dave Murgatroyd (Radcliffe Borough), Dave Murray (Trafford), Jim Davies (Waterloo Dock), and Rob Turley (West Didsbury & Chorlton).

I am also grateful to Alice Lock and Yvonne Young at Tameside Archives, Kath Lapsley at Manchester Central Library, and to Andrew Lee-Hart at Crosby Library. Richard Rundle`s Football Club History Database (www.fchd.btinternet.com) is a superb historical resouce and has helped me enormously.

Finally I would like to dedicate this book to those who work so hard and sacrifice so much of their own time, effort and money to keep alive so many of the clubs featured. One of the very first clubs I visited was Castleton Gabriels (now Rochdale Town). I was welcomed by Club Secretary Jim Picken who had been there early getting the ground ready for the match, who entertained visitors whilst his wife (the Club Treasurer) made sandwiches, who sold programmes that the Picken family had produced, and who manned the turnstile. Jim also acted as Commercial Manager, and it`s probably no exaggeration to say that the club would not have existed today but for the work of Jim and his family in the early years of this century. There are Jim Pickens in so many clubs – to all of you, many thanks!

Terry Gorman
January 2009

Ashton United F.C.

**Hurst Cross, Surrey Street,
Ashton-under-Lyne,
OL6 8DY**

Originally a distinct village outside Ashton-under-Lyne, Hurst has long been absorbed into the town. Hurst Cross is one of the oldest non-league grounds still being used in Lancashire, with probably the most fascinating and complex history of all.

Sadly its future is uncertain, and there is a reluctance to spend significant sums of money because of this. The uncertainty revolves around the new Tameside Stadium, and pressure from Tameside Council for Ashton United to join Curzon Ashton as joint residents. The Board have a balancing act between ground grading requirements and prudence. The situation is complicated because Curzon Ashton are already in residence at the new stadium,

and would be the senior partner. Like so many clubs at this level, the main source of income is the social club, which also serves as a community centre in Hurst Cross, so whether or not it would be feasible for United to keep its social income in the immediate area but play on the other side of Ashton is something that only time will tell.

The original date of the ground is still being researched by club historian Jez Sayle, but he has discovered a record of a game played between Hurst and Hurst Red Star in March 1879. Whilst the venue is not specified, the post-match social was held in the Hare and Hounds which still stands opposite the present ground. The landlord of the other pub opposite, the Church Inn, subsequently built a changing room and installed a billiards table for the club's use – and the Church Inn is also still there.

The Lees Road end in the 1980s.
Photo: Ashton United F.C.

The former side cover. Photo: Andy Dakin

The age of the ground is well reflected in its setting – enclosed by terraced streets with council housing built on what had been the cricket pitch. There is a slope wing to wing which drops away from the main stand.

The interesting miscellany of buildings along the main stand side of the ground reflects the reluctance to invest until the future is clear. At one end is the social club which extends into the Directors and Sponsors lounge from which the privileged get an excellent view. In front of this are potted plants and picnic ta-

bles for the odd Summer day. The main stand is a tall, four bay structure with a pent roof, surmounted by 11 flags flying proudly. This replaced the original stand dating from 1912, shown in Andy Dakin's photo, which had become unsafe. Further along this side of the ground there is a selection of different wooden buildings and portakabins, which contain the refreshment bar, the club shop, and the club office. The turnstiles are in that corner.

Below: The cover on the far side under construction in the early 1990s.

Photo: Tameside Archives

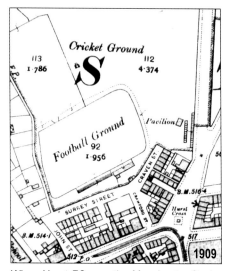

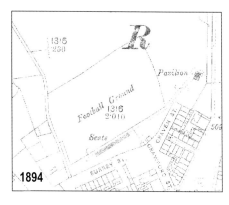

When Hurst FC won the Manchester Senior Cup at Hurst Cross in 1885 (beating Newton Heath Lancashire & Yorkshire Railway – later to become Manchester United) the toast at the celebratory dinner was "*The Hurst Cricket and Football Club*". Interestingly, the OS map frrom 1894 shows the football pitch with seated area, and a separate pavilion but without showing the cricket pitch, whereas the 1909 map shows the same pavilion, but located on a clearly marked cricket pitch.

Hurst FC folded in 1892, and the pitch was taken over by Hurst Ramblers who played in The Combination and then the Lancashire Combination. They in turn folded in season 1899/1900 and their record was expunged. In 1909 a new Hurst FC was formed.

The ground was used throughout WWII as it was taken over by an Army XI playing in the Manchester League from 1942 onwards. Over the years there has also been baseball, American football, and rugby league played on the ground. In 1947 the club changed to its present name.

Ashton United's former stand. Photo: Andy Dakin

Opposite the main stand is an 8 bay terrace with five steps built at the beginning of the 1990`s, and there is no cover at either end of the ground. The floodlights are rather unusual - the eight pylons are not regularly spaced. The end pylons are at the edge of the penalty area, the others fitted where the existing buildings permit. The club's current safety certificate is for a crowd of 2,500, compared with the 11,000 who saw the FA Cup First Round game against Halifax in 1952. The Hurst Cross ground is part of our social history – it would be dreadful for it to disappear.

Above, left: The attractive patio area by the Officials Room.
Above: The stand proudly flies a magnificent range of flags.

Below: The view from the covered terrace.
Below, left: The Lees Road end today.

The delightfully traditional setting of Hurst Cross with the hills just visible in the distance.

Mossley F.C.
Seel Park,
Market Street,
Mossley, OL5 0ES

I n so many ways Seel Park shares common features with many Pennine ex-mill town grounds, and yet could never be anything other than itself. Fortunately I have a number of photos from Tameside Archives and from John Cawthorne the club historian to supplement my own.

The history of the ground's development is almost worthy of a book in itself. The club was formed in 1903, and played under a couple of names before becoming Mossley in 1909, moving to what was called Seel Fold from Luzley, which was originally a rugby ground with open seating.

John believes that this was in 1911, but over the years the date has 'evolved' into 1912, which is now the officially accepted version. The name was changed in 1931 to Seel Park

Above: The corner at the lowest point of the ground, with restricted access around to the covered terrace.

as that was deemed more "modern" than Fold.

The club's headquarters were initially in the Highland Laddie Hotel next to the ground, and the first stand was built in 1920 with cover for 430, actually on the opposite side to today's main stand. This was extended in 1927 to cover 1000, and Mossley Co-operative Society erected 'refreshment buildings'. In 1932 a new main stand was built on the Market Street side of the ground, and the players` tunnel was incorporated into this. It survived until badly damaged in a storm in 1987.

Much of what you see at Seel Park today was funded by the sale of players during the club's very successful 1970's – Alan Roberts to Bradford Park Avenue, Gary Pierce to Huddersfield Town and Eamonn O`Keefe to Everton.

The ground itself stands just below the crest of a hill, on land where levelling efforts have been made – but without having been overly successful. Approached through turnstiles opened officially in 1952 you cross a car park to the bars and social clubs, etc, between which there are narrow passageways to give access to the pitch, and also to stunning views across onto Pennine moorland. In front of these facilities are rather splendid terraces, and then sloping terracing down to pitch level. On the half-way line on this side is the smart pent-roofed stand erected to replace the damaged one, although not quite as long, and so the old players` tunnel remains, but at the side

Above: The old main stand. Photo: Mossley F.C. Below: Construction of the new stand with the old players' tunnel still in situ.

Photo: Tameside Archives

of it – providing an impenetrable obstacle to spectators wishing to walk around the pitch. In fact, a diversion has to be made around the back of the stand if you want access to the far end without walking all around the pitch.

Storm damage in 1987. Photo: Tameside Archives

In the corner near the entrance is the club shop, and then behind the goal is an area of covered terracing. The ground boundaries close right in on the corner, and then there is new tiered terracing on the far touchline, on either side of covered standing accommodation which simply had a sloping dirt floor. Behind the second goal there is no cover.

If you ask which way the pitch slopes, the answer would almost be, "every way". The touch line along the half in front of the clubs and bars is almost level, although the pitch drops away towards the opposite touchline, but the other half climbs quite steeply up from the half way line, but again drops away towards the opposite side. There is quite a severe drop diagonally from corner to corner.

Below: The Park End and the social club seen from the Popular Side.

But the folk of Mossley are obviously proud of their club – everything is spotless and well-painted and crowds tend to be above the divisional average, despite what was a not very good season at the time of our visit. The record is 6,640 on 19th April, 1946, for a 1-1 Cheshire League draw against local rivals, Stalybridge Celtic.

Below: The Park End stand funded by the sale of Eamonn O'Keefe.

2007

Photo: Mossley F.C.   1952

Above & top: Admission in 2007 is £7, but was just 1/- (5p) when the new turnstiles were opened in 1952. *Above, left*: The floor under the cover where the main stand once stood had not been flagged at the time of my visit. *Left*: Either side of this cover is terracing laid with paving slabs.

The Pennines seen from the entrance over the top of the covered terrace.

Droylsden F.C.
**Butchers Arms Ground,
Market Street,
Droylsden, M43 7AW**

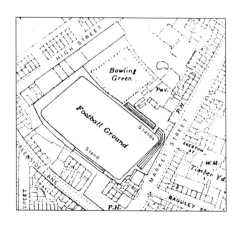

Droylsden seem to have been the 19th Century equivalents of Wigan Robin Park. Apparently Thomas Cropper, the landlord of the Butchers Arms pub in Droylsden had a field behind his hostelry and in 1892 invited football enthusiasts to form a team to play on it. The field was then known as the Droylsden Wakes Ground as it had long been used as the location for the Droylsden Wakes Fair, held over an extended weekend every August. It would seem that Mr Cropper was quite an entrepreneur, for not only did he oversee the birth of the football club, but he also had a bowling green, and the fair continued using the field for another twenty years after the football team started using it. The 1933 OS map shows the way the area was laid out at that time, with the "PH" being the Butchers Arms.

The club joined the Manchester & District Allaince in 1894 and progressed rapidly. Droylsden played Hyde United in the 1921 Manchester Junior Cup Final at National Park (see p. 80) in front of a crowd of 15,000. The stadium was developed progressively, with a new stand being built in the 1929/30 season, thanks mainly to the generosity of the Openshaw Brewery Company. Over that season the average gate had been 400, and the club finished the season with a profit of £3.

By 1933 the capacity of the ground was estimated to be 8,000 with covered stands for 2,500. A number of non-football events such as boxing matches were held on the playing area, and although designed to raise funds to improve the ground, they contributed to the pitch being renowned for its lack of grass.

In 1936 the club was elected to the Lancashire Combination, and the club put a lot of effort into the pitch itself and into further improving the ground, including the construction of a new 800 seater stand along the touchline at the Greenside Lane side of the ground. The following season Droylsden became for a time a nursery club to Manchester City, whose A Team played at the Butchers Arms. 'Surplus' City players were used by Droylsden, which led to their disqualification from the FA Cup.

Above: A wonderful shot of the old main stand. Photo: Dave Siddall

Complications set in after WWII when the lease of the ground was sold to Belle Vue FC who renamed themselves Droylsden United, and Droylsden were forced to play at the Moorside Trotting Stadium until the local council bought the ground, and negotiated a shotgun marriage between the two apparently quite bitter rivals.

The old side cover.

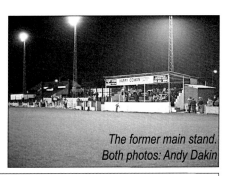

The former main stand. Both photos: Andy Dakin

The ground as it was in the 1960s. Photo: Tameside Archives

In 1951 Droylsden returned to a renovated ground where the pitch had been rotated to its present position – at the expense of the bowling green - and a long-standing drainage problem cured. At that stage they took Droylsden United`s place in the Lancashire Combination, returning to the Cheshire County League in 1968.

At the beginning of the 1970s the club came under pressure from the Cheshire League to erect floodlights so that kick-offs in Winter did not have to be so early that attendances suffered. Droylsden had a major campaign for fundraising, with games against Leeds, Man City and Man Utd. Don Revie personally switched the lights on in 1971.

Above: The roof of the side terrace, also seen below, is of exceptionally solid construction.

Under Dave Pace, Chairman and Manager since the 1990s, the club has grown and developed at a tremendous rate. The photos show the development of the ground, with the old main stand compared with the new and what was the open Greenside Lane end where the 1936 stand had been demolished, but is now a covered terrace. Nonetheless, the pitch is tightly hemmed in between Market Street and housing. In fact, in one corner the gap between the pitch perimeter fence and the external fencing is so small that two adults cannot pass through side by side.

On the Market Street side of the ground is the new brick stand, under which are offices and changing rooms. Alongside this is the imposing Phoenix Social Club. On the side opposite the stand is the most wonderful timber-framed covered terrace – built from baulks of timber of almost railway sleeper proportions. With a current capacity of 3,000, the post war ground record is 4250 against Grimsby in the FA Cup First Round in 1976.

Above: The Greenside Lane end beyond the side terrace.
Below: The clubhouse in the 1960s.

Marine F.C.

Rossett Park, College Road,
Crosby,
L23 3AS

This has got to be one of my all-time favourite grounds – at least it was until the ground was renamed in a sponsorship deal. Why else name a football ground after a bus company? The history of name changes suggests that the traditional name will eventually be used again so I use it here.

On their website, Marine proudly quote one of the club's early officials, who said that, "Marine Football Club was founded in 1894 by a few well-known gentlemen of the district meeting at the Marine Hotel in Waterloo". In other words this was never a mere pub team, but a club which used to have a reputation for exclusivity. Originally playing at Waterloo Park, they moved to their present ground in 1904.

From College Road the ground is easy to

spot, as is the entrance for season ticket or pass holders. It is less easy for paying spectators who eventually locate the turnstiles and find themselves in a ginnel between the gardens of houses in Jubilee Road and the changing block. This feeling of narrowness pervades the whole ground, as it is sandwiched between Jubilee Road and Rossett Road. In fact, sandwiched is a euphemistic way of putting it.

There is an excellent history of the club and ground in the club's centenary book, written by club President and Historian, Dave Wotherspoon, who told me that originally there were two pitches laid end to end between the two roads, with the ground running as far as the railway line.

Covered standing accommodation at the College Road end was built in the 1920s, and in the 1930s the club sold the far pitch to a developer. He built houses on a road he called Crosender Road (after which that end of the ground is named today) and a stand was built on that newly closed end.

In this most traditional of grounds even the modern cantilevered stand looks in keeping behind one goal.

The Crosender Road end stand.
Photo: Andy Dakin

The Crosender Road End stand was only removed nine years ago, leaving simply uncovered terracing, split into three blocks, with an emergency exit gate at the rear. The earlier College Road End cover was removed and partially replaced by a modern cantilever 400-seater stand opened in February 2000, with uncovered terracing along the rest of that end, but with a passageway between the two for access to the Scouse House – the corrugated-iron roofed refreshment hut.

Current plans include a new cover over the Crosender Road End and also for a turnstile entrance from Crosender Road for occasional use with unusually large crowds. Without this turnstile, the only access to that end is down one side of the pitch through a narrow covered terrace which just about has room for two rows of spectators between the touchline and the Jubilee Road gardens` wall. The floodlight pylons poke through the roof of this structure.

The former College Road stand
Photo: Andy Dakin

Prior to Marine joining the Northern Premier League, spectators were also permitted on the Rossett Road side. Their eventual election to the NPL was conditional upon creating more space between the sidelines and the rails, so the whole pitch was moved sideways towards Rossett Road, and spectator access to that side was closed.

This means that the touchline is very close to the gardens of Rossett Road and there is just about room to squeeze in a couple of dug-outs. The floodlight pylons on this side of the pitch are close to the sidelines and so the lower parts are covered in padding to protect the players.

A wonderful touch is the house numbers on the fences along both side-lines, so that club officials can keep track of which house to knock at to retrieve balls that disappear during a game.

The record crowd is 4,000 in 1949 for a friendly against Nigeria during their tour which included the inauguration of the South Liverpool floodlights. Capacity is now 3,185 (another of those remarkably precise figures). Unfortunately the three-sided nature of the ground means that there is no way the club could satisfy the grading requirements for Step 2, whatever their league position.

Photo: David Wotherspoon

Above: The Rossett Road side with spectator access. *Below*: Spectators cannot watch from this side of the ground today.

Below: The narrow terracing on the Jubilee Road side. *Below, left*: The Jubilee Road side seen from the Crosender Road terrace.

Atherton Collieries F.C.
Alder Street
Atherton,
M46 9FJ

The clubhouse in 1999.Photo: Mike Floate

I first visited this ground a couple of years before starting on the book, and it was really run down and suffering from vandalism. Consequently when the Club Secretary's response to the news that I would be visiting to take photos for the book was a request not to take photos of some of the problem areas, I was prepared for the worst yet I am delighted to note that things were much improved since my previous visit.

Very close to the centre of Atherton, the ground has a long history, being originally part of the miners` welfare club which catered for those who worked in the 6 or 7 pits in the Atherton area. In use by the club since its foundation in 1916, the pitch was originally at

90 degrees to the current layout, and apparently a bowling green was sacrificed in the re-orientation. There is now a slope down from end to end. The changing rooms are behind the goal at the top of the ground, separate from the wooden clubhouse on the opposite side of the pitch to the turnstiles. Whilst the clubhouse roof may not be the straightest in this world, the building is well-maintained. Recently an extension to the roof has removed a further small seated area, which can be seen in the photo above.

Also on the clubhouse side are two simple covered seating areas which look as though they ought to be joined as one.

On the opposite side of the pitch is a covered standing area, with the remains of vandalised seats at the back. Behind the home dugout is some concrete terracing that was once a wonderfully individual home-built covered terrace (photo below). The lower end of the ground has no cover, just a vintage open-roofed gents urinal in one corner.

Above: Twin covers on the clubhouse side in 1999. Photo: Mike Floate
Below: The side covers in 2008.

The record crowd is said to be 3300 for a Lancashire Combination game in the 1920`s. This is a friendly club, let's hope they win their battle against the vandals.

Proudly displaying the club stripes, the two covered terraces in 1999. Photo: Mike Floate

Atherton Laburnum Rovers F.C.
Crilly Park, Spa Road,
Atherton,
M46 9FB

I n 1966 Atherton LR moved into their current home, which is named after a previous Chairman who died suddenly in 1980. The club was founded in 1956 by Joe Riley for his younger brother and friends to play league football. They began playing on the council's Laburnum Playing Fields – hence their initial name of Laburnum Rovers. Their subsequent Norfolk Road home, where they played from 1960 to 1965, was also a park pitch.

Eventually they acquired their own site, although considerable work - well recorded on their website – was necessary to get the field and pond they took over into reasonable condition. The club got approval to use it in 1966 at an annual rent of two guineas (£2-20). At that time the ground was simply known as Spa Road.

When the team joined the Cheshire County League in 1980, they had to add Atherton to their name.

Approached either through turnstiles directly off the road or through their own fenced car park, the ground slopes from goal to goal down towards the railway. Dominated by a modern 250 capacity cantilever stand built during the 1993/4 season, there is covered standing accommodation on the opposite touchline. Earlier photos show that this was originally two separate roofs, with a gap between in which the dug-outs were located. These have now been moved to the opposite touchline, and the gap has been filled in with a roof which is higher and at a different pitch from its two neighbours.

There is no cover at the top of the slope, and at the lower end the cover is sufficiently far from the pitch to be used as storage for ground maintenance equipment.

The whole set-up is a credit to the club, and possibly suggests that opening the clubhouse every night is one way of reducing vandalism – although many of the plastic seats originally installed in the new stand were vandalised.

Record attendance is 2300 for an FA Vase Quarter Final Replay against Aldershot Town in season 1993/94.

Behind the fence on the opposite side of the pitch to the stand is an area currently gone wild which is part of the complex, and on which the club plans to develop a couple of small pitches for youngsters.

Below: The top goal.

Above: The clubhouse located in the corner at the bottom end of the pitch. *Below*: The turnstiles are in the northeast corner. *Bottom*: The three sections comprising the covered terrace are found opposite the main stand.

Bootle F.C.
New Bucks Park, Vestey Road,
off Bridle Road, Bootle,
L30 4UN

Situated at the end of an upmarket commercial estate cul-de-sac off Bridle Road in Bootle, the ground is distinguished by a large wind turbine in front of the car park. As a landmark, it's quite noticeable.

The history of Bootle-titled football clubs is complex and confusing. In summary, the original Bootle, started in 1880 and founder members of the Second Division of the Football League in 1882, folded after one season. A new club, Bootle Athletic eventually took over their ground in Hawthorne Road, but folded during season 1953/4.

Coincidentally, Langton FC was formed in 1953 by the employees of Langton Dock in Bootle, and as one of a dozen docks-based teams in Liverpool at that time they played at the Dockers Club in Edinburgh Park until 1973. They then changed their name to Bootle FC and for five seasons played at Orrell Mount Park before creating Bucks Park on the Northern Perimeter Road for season 1978/9. It was there that they became founder members of the NWCFL. The demise of that ground is described in the Gone section later, and left the club homeless although with money from the sale of the lease.

Season 2000/2001 found the club playing at Kirkby Sports Centre, but relegated to Division 2 because the Centre did not have floodlights. Subsequently the gym in the building was condemned, and so it wasn't possible to use the changing rooms underneath them, which led to the NWCFL excluding Bootle completely. The Centre was closed at short notice for urgent work in 2002 – and never reopened.

Below: A wind turbine stands by the entrance - a good landmark when finding the ground.

Despite a lot of looking – and having cash in the bank – the club was unable to find a site to establish a stadium to meet NWCFL requirements, and so they played in the Liverpool Combination, ground sharing with Waterloo Dock back at the Edinburgh Park Dockers Club for one season and then at the Civil Service ground in Drummond Road for three.

The search for a place to set up their own home continued, and they were rewarded by the offer of a long-term lease on land newly acquired by Sefton Council. They moved in – and back into the NWCFL in 2006. I suppose it's sad that I should be surprised about a council being so helpful to their local non-league club – but good on Sefton.

When first they moved in, the club made use of portakabins, but tired of waiting for grants and spent time and money replacing these with more permanent structures. The clubhouse and changing room block have been built. There are two standard-issue portable terrace units, one with seats to comply with NWCFL requirements positioned near the corner, the second acting as a covered terrace behind one goal.

The two dugouts are both on the opposite side of the pitch to the changing rooms, and on the far side of those is a decent-sized training area. It is an individual ground despite everything. The only difficulty seems to be pitch drainage, as they had to cancel a number of home games in 2007/8. Apparently 85% of the playing surface drains perfectly, but 15% is compacted and holds water. When I spoke to Secretary Joe Doran the club were in the midst of work to rectify the problem.

Above: A standard prefabricated seated area satisfies grading requirements but lacks character.

Below: A second unit serves fans better as a terrace behind one goal.

Right: The wind turbine stands just outside the entrance to the ground.

Chadderton F.C.
Andrew Street,
Chadderton,
OL9 0JT

The club was formed in 1947 as Millbrow Football Club, becoming North Chadderton Amateurs before adopting the current name in 1957. Founder members of the NWCFL in 1982, they originally played at Mill Brow but moved to Andrew Street for season 1954/55, creating the pitch from scratch. The pitch was originally much nearer the road but when that was widened in 1971 was moved 50 yards to the east. There was a lot of work to level the new playing area, and the surplus earth means that the end furthest

Above: The Officials' section within the covered side terrace.

from the clubhouse is banked quite steeply almost immediately after the goal line.

The original clubhouse was destroyed by fire, along with most of the club's historical records, and replaced with the current brick building. There is a low covered terrace/stand along the Broadway perimeter, with a wonderful separate section for "Officials". This is the only covered accommodation. With a listed capacity of 2500, the ground record is 1500 for a game against Guiness Exports in 1969.

Unfortunately the club was relegated to the NWCFL Division 2 in 1998 due to the ground failing the grading being applied by the NWCFL as it worked to establish itself as part of Level Six of the National Football Pyramid.

Chadderton's problem is that the ground is not on a long-term lease. It is owned by Oldham Council and classed as public open space, though the Council make no contribution towards the upkeep. Therefore the club cannot lock its own gate, and there is constant vandalism from people who congregate in the stand at night. The only other people taking advantage of this open space are apparently dog-walkers taking their pets in the ground.

Right: The solid brick clubhouse is sadly no match for local vandals.

The club was taken over in 2007 by Craig Halliwell and Tony Bhatti who had ambitious plans to renovate the place and improve the facilities. In fact they started on this work, and for health and safety reasons locked the gates whilst the work was carried out. One of the dog-walkers complained, the local councillor took up his case, the club was forced to unlock them – and almost immediately the clubhouse was broken into and badly damaged three times within a couple of weeks. The club's two owners subsequently said that they would seriously have to consider relocating if the council insisted on the ground being kept unlocked. Quite rightly, they were unwilling to invest in the club if they could not take action to protect the work done. An outcome was not known as we went to press.

The covered side has a central area with seats and single step terracing to both ends.

Curzon Ashton F.C.
The Tameside Stadium,
Richmond Street,
Ashton-under-Lyne, OL7 9HG

The home of Curzon Ashton FC and of Ashton Curzon Ladies FC was opened for the start of the 2005/2006 season. Built by Tameside Metropolitan Borough Council (the initials of which are picked out in the seats in the main stand) and leased to Curzon Ashton on a 99 year lease, the Council's original objective was to make the new stadium the home of both Curzon Ashton and Ashton United. For a number of reasons this ground-share failed to come to fruition, and apparently the Council then tried to attract Droylsden to become tenants. This also failed, but the Council's Corporate Plan still has a clear objective about attracting a second club to share the ground. A complicating political (with a small "p") factor is that Curzon Ashton, as first resident, would probably be the senior partner in any such arrangement. As it is, the Curzon Ashton groundstaff maintain the pitch.

The stadium won an award as 'Best New Non-League Ground' from Groundtastic magazine in 2005, and the arena is a great set-up and a tribute to the local council.

On the side of the pitch away from Ashton town centre is a simple covered terraced without sides, and facing it is the new main stand which incorporates excellent hospitality facilities and changing rooms.

In addition there are further changing rooms, for between Ashton and that main stand is a third generation artificial pitch which is in regular use by the local community. In their first season at the ground, Curzon Ashton Reserves played on that, until the Cheshire League decided that because it did not have a rail or a rope around the playing surface, they would have to use the main pitch instead.

There are a couple of particularly interesting points of note. Firstly, at the changing room end of the players` tunnel is a magnificent plaque bearing the coat of arms of Ashton. Provided by the local council from one of the old municipal buildings, this has been cleaned, painted, turned into a club crest, and mounted on the wall.

The other intriguing point that struck me is the provision of two turnstile entrances at each corner of the ground, even though one corner seems to open only onto a field – obviously planning for the future.

Above & right: The cover on the far side has a roof which is designed to match the roof of the main stand rather than to give protection to those sheltering under it.

Curzon Ashton was formed in 1963 by the merger of two clubs. The "Curzon" comes from Curzon Road FC (which apparently was previously Curzon Road Methodists FC), and the "Ashton" is almost from Assheton (sic) Amateurs FC. By one of those strange co-incidences, the latter used to play on a park pitch which lies just outside the new stadium complex. Until 2004 the newly merged club played at National Park (see p. 80), originally the home of Ashton National FC, and now gone. They played the season 2004/5 at Stalybridge Celtic whilst their new ground was being completed.

Photo: Colin Peel

Below: The main stand with terracing built to a good height alongside.

Daisy Hill F.C.
New Sirs, St James Street,
Westhoughton, Bolton,
BL5 2EB

Daisy Hill is a suburb of Westhoughton, itself an outlying suburb of Bolton. Lying in the midst of a pleasant residential area, and off the beaten track, the entrance to the ground is quite hard to find, with a gravel track well concealed between the drives of two adjacent houses. The club house is a long, low building, with a corrugated roof showing the signs of age, and fixtures and admission prices are chalked up on a blackboard near the turnstile, acquired by the club secretary from Hampden Park.

Founded in 1894 as Daisy Hill St James, the club owes its origins to the church just up the road, but dropped the "St James" before the end of WWI. It has been in existence ever since, apart from the six or seven years it took to restart after the Second World War. In 1989 it changed name to Westhoughton Town, but reverted to Daisy Hill in 1994. Over the years the club has played on a number of pitches

in the area, and between the two wars they played on the other side of the neighbouring cricket club, having to "borrow" a few yards from the cricketers to give themselves a full size pitch. They moved to New Sirs in 1958 – but Secretary Bob Naylor tells us that it is strongly rumoured that they had previously played there in the early years of the Twentieth Century. "New Sirs" is said to derive from the family which held land in the area for many years – the Le Sires. At one stage the family built another farm cottage for a son, and the land associated with the new farm became New Sirs.

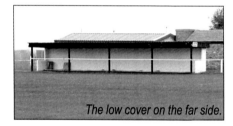

The low cover on the far side.

The club house runs parallel to one end of the pitch, and has a covered seating area , with wonderful wooden seats which were originally in the main stand at Blackburn Rovers' Ewood Park. They were taken out when Blackburn created their first executive boxes and bought by Daisy Hill secretary Bob Naylor. Each one was individually sponsored with a brass name plate, but sadly most have been stolen. The tea bar is located in the middle of this, and is notable for serving drinks in mugs, rather than those awful plastic or polystyrene cups.

The home and away dug-outs are on opposite sides of the pitch, with a low covered standing area to the side of the home bench. When I say, "Low", I mean it, and there is a "Mind Your Head" sign to warn unaware spectators.

The half nearer to the club house is flanked by the gardens of adjacent houses, while there is a pitch for junior sides beyond a fence beside the other half.

Other interesting features include fencing at either end which is curved around behind the goals, and the hard standing around much of the pitch is actually deliberately laid crazy paving. This reflects just a little of the devotion and effort that so many people have put into keeping Daisy Hill in existence over the years, despite suffering badly from vandalism, at one stage having their mower torched.

The record crowd is "about 2000" for the Westhoughton Charity Cup Final against Horwich RMI in May 1980. The club still plays in the NWCFL of which they were founder members.

Above: *A further view of the clubhouse and associated seating area.*
Below: *The ex Blackburn Rovers seating.*

Above: *Seating at the clubhouse end.*
Below: *A simple barrier spoils the view but satifies ground grading requirements.*

Flixton F.C.

Valley Road,
Flixton,
M41 8RQ

Quite difficult to find, the Valley Road ground nestles on the edge of a large housing estate just before the no-mans land that leads down to the Manchester Ship Canal. An easy way of finding it is to look for the clearing in the midst of the forest of pylons - it was quite difficult to get any photos which did not include one or more of the high voltage pylons which surround the pitch.

It really is an interesting ground in many ways. The initial approach is through a gateway into a narrow car park which also accommodates the premises of a taxi firm. There is a turn-stile on that side of the ground, but things are complicated because the very large and ac-tive clubhouse is at the far, Ship Canal side of the pitch, and there is also an entrance there. Once into the ground, the most noticeable feature is that the changing rooms are on the opposite side of the pitch to the clubhouse.

The clubhouse (see photo above) is close to the playing area and has its own balcony. It takes up most of one half, with a four row stand which is even closer taking up most of the other. The Officials` part of the stand is close to the half-way line and has three rows of seats with the PA/Press Box behind. Like many other such stands, the main path around the pitch runs between it and the pitch wall – but the closeness means that this pathway is so narrow that it discourages spectators from standing there and blocking the view.

On the opposite side of the pitch is a covered standing area which runs the full length of the pitch. As the ground boundary is so close to the gardens of the neighbouring houses, this covered area is very narrow – particularly behind the dug-outs.

Both ends are uncovered, and there is a shed which presumably houses the electrics behind each of the goals. Andy Dakin`s earlier photos shows the Ship Canal side of the pitch (and a few of the pylons) before the clubhouse and new stand were built. With a current ground limit of 2,000, record attendance is 1,543 for an FA Vase Semi-Final with Brigg Town in season 1995/6.

When I visited I was told that work was planned to put a further layer of soil on the pitch, particularly down the centre line between the goals as it is apparently rather lower in the middle of the park than down the wings.

Above: The main stand.

Above: A simple, shallow cover on one side.

The officials section of the stand.

Early cover on the Ship Canal side before the stand and clubhouse were built. Photo: Andy Dakin

The standing cover on the Flixton side. Photo: Andy Dakin

Formby F.C.
Altcar Road,
Formby,
L37 8DL

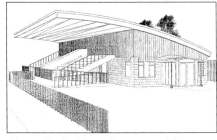

I t's interesting how nice people can make you think kindly of their club, despite the state of their facilities, and it's equally possible for not very nice people to jaundice your view of an interesting stadium. Formby was an exception to this rule. I met lovely folk at the ground, but despite that all I can say is that Altcar Lane was a dreadfully uninspiring place. It was a sad far cry from the words of optimism in the last Brows Lane programme of the then manager Peter Henerty, "If everything goes to plan we will end up with one of the best grounds in the North West with potential for further expansion…….."

The club left Brows Lane, their home for the previous 82 years, and moved here for the 2002/3 season. The notice they had been given to move was too short to meet the

Above: Sadly this earlier proposal for a new stand was not built.

NWCLFL ground grading deadline so the club played the season in the Liverpool County Combination for the first time for 34 years. Whilst 2003/4 saw them return to the North West Counties, the £175,000 they had been given as part of the move was insufficient to build the proposed new facilities. The good fortune was that they gained promotion in their first season back – albeit as a result of league restructuring. That season also saw the highest crowd at Altcar Lane, when 602 watched Formby v Southport in the Liverpool Senior Cup.

Next door to the local municipal waste disposal site, it certainly looks as though the dividing line between the two isn't totally respected, and the approach to the ground is not the neatest and cleanest. The perimeter fencing to the ground is unusual in being wooden on two sides but open mesh fencing on the other two. Entering through the one open turnstile in a corner of the ground, immediately on your right there is a collection of disparate containers and portakabins which are the changing rooms and facilities. A very homely refreshment cabin with separate 'Officials' room, which was moved from Brows Lane, completes this assembly.

There is a dugout at each side of the pitch, with the concrete pitch enclosure wall built round them, to give an almost moat-like effect. Behind the home dugout there is an elevated glass fronted cabin which is presumably for the media. On the day of our visit, however, it was full of rubbish, including the remnants of a broken garden bench. Behind the goal at the far end is a wooden covered standing area.

Right & right lower: The dugout, pitch wall and media room.
Below: The rather uninspiring entrance to Altcar Lane.

There is a matching covered area to the left of the turnstile corner, this time with the obligatory seats. For some reason this is not centrally located behind the goal, but offset.

The whole set-up appeared to suggest that very little had been spent on the ground since the club had moved in, and subsequent events seem to support this supposition. In May 2008, rumours suggested that the club was considering moving again, as the lack of a licensed club at the ground was causing them financial problems. The plan under consideration was to create a new stadium associated with a country club near the beach, but this fell through. Subsequently major disagreements resulted in the resignations of club officials, and the club was sold in July 2008. The aim of the new owners is said to be to turn it into much more of a general sports facility including tennis courts and an all-weather pitch.

Irlam F.C.
Silver Street,
Irlam,
M44 6JL

Above: Irlam Town, 1989. Photo: Andy Dakin

Silver Street is truly another phoenix risen from the ashes. For many years it was the pitch of Irlam Town AFC, formed in 1965 and who played at Silver Street from that date. They joined the Cheshire League from the Manchester League in 1978, and became one of the founder members of the NWCFL, where they played for three seasons before spending five in the Northern Premier League's new Division One. They then returned to Division Two of the NWCFL for another three until they were removed from the League in 1995 because they failed to meet grading standards, apparently because of the state of the clubhouse and the ground. As a consequence, the club disbanded.

The side cover in 1989.Photo: Andy Dakin

Below: The old Irlam Town clubhouse.

The abandoned facilities became a vandal's delight, and were torched on a number of occasions. The local council flattened the whole place – clubhouse and changing rooms - and it became simply a park pitch which would have merited inclusion in the Gone section.

Enter Mitchell & Shackleton FC, originally a works team based in Eccles. Their ground had been taken over for redevelopment, but leaving them with funds for relocation. In 2001, they added Irlam to their name and became Irlam Mitchell & Shackleton FC. With their own funding and a Football Foundation grant, they worked hard at developing the ground from the open pitch they inherited, opening their new changing room block in 2003. Featured on the ground at present is a direction sign to Irlam Town FC that was still on the main road nearby when they took over the site.

Above: Standing cover by one corner, more individual than the nearby portable seated area.
Below: Three photos showing the strange dugouts at Silver Street.

Subsequently the club decided to drop the factory name, and became simply Irlam FC in 2006. However, they are still working hard at developing their ground, and as we went to print it was confirmed that they had been elected to the NWCFL for season 2008/9. A cover has been built over standing accommodation behind the goal nearer to the changing rooms, improved floodlights fitted on new pylons, and the small ubiquitous prefabricated stand installed. Just before the start of the 2008/9 season the ground was unique in having 14 floodlight pylons – the original six and the improved eight. The plan is to remove the three old ones on the Silver Street touchline, and to turn the old three on the opposite side to illuminate the training pitch over the fence. A social club is also to be constructed between the entrance gate and the changing room block.

The most notable features of the place are the splendid dugouts – constructed around bus shelters, and made to be as vandal-proof as possible. At the time of our first visit the Club Secretary was fighting a valiant but losing battle against moles which had taken possession of one of his penalty areas. Since then he has subcontracted that task.

Maine Road F.C.

Brantingham Road,
Chorlton-cum-Hardy,
M21 0TT

The ground belongs to the local church and was originally known as St Margaret's Playing Fields. In the 1970s the pitch had been used by Anson Villa who played a couple of seasons in the Cheshire County League before amalgamating with Salford Amateurs who played at Moor Lane.

Brantingham Road then became the home of the Manchester FA, and the pitch was their County Ground. Recently the FA wanted to expand their offices but there was reluctance on the church's part to extend the lease which expires at the end of 2008. The FA then relocated to Salford Sports Village.

Maine Road FC started as a Manchester City supporters` team, playing on Hough End park pitches, before playing in Failsworth at Tootal's ground, and then in Stockport. In 1986 they moved to Brantingham Road as tenants of the FA. Initially the changing facilities were in prefabs, but during that season the FA built their office/changing room complex, which met NWCFL grading requirements, so Maine Road were admitted to the League for season 1987/88.

Whilst the Maine Road club's record crowd is 3,151 against FC United of Manchester, that game was played at Stalybridge Celtic's ground, and the Brantingham Road record is apparently 875 against Altrincham in the FA Cup in 1990. Theoretical capacity is 2,000.

As the Manchester FA do not have a County Pitch in the new Sports Village, a number of games such as local cup semi-finals are still played on the old County Ground.

Left: The cover further from the clubhouse.

The church apparently wish to use some of the land to extend their school premises, and so the short life of the remaining lease, combined with its previous role as HQ of the Manchester FA leaves a first class building/changing room facility, an excellent playing surface, but with spectator facilities that have not been touched for some time. The best illustration of this was an advert on one of the covered seating areas for the Manchester Evening News Pink - that had not been published for at least two seasons at the time of our visit.

The turnstile entrance is of a standard that reflects the ground's past use for cup and representative games, and is at one end of the pitch.

There are covered spectator facilities down both touchlines – on the left two separate covered enclosures with seats, and the dugouts in between, and on the right a covered terrace with both seats and standing areas along most of the side of the pitch. Both ends are uncovered.

Derek Barber, the Secretary of Maine Road, has been assured by the church that they will not be summarily thrown off Brantingham Road, but its future is obviously in some doubt.

Above: A view of the side cover.
Below: Simple bench seating within the far cover.

Above: The clubhouse and the cover nearest the entrance.
Below: A close-up view of the same cover.

Oldham Borough F.C.

White Bank Stadium, White Bank Road, Hollins, Oldham, OL8 3JH

Oldham Borough started in 1964 as the works team of George Dew, a major building contractor. The club was known as Oldham Dew until 1985 when they became Oldham Town, and they created their present stadium in 1992/3.

The previous ground at Nordens Road was used for filming the BBC Children's series "Jossy's Giants".

They took over the open pitch and large clubhouse that had been used by Chamber Colliery in the Manchester Amateur League. As good neighbours, they let Castleton Gabriels play at White Bank to avoid them being relegated from the NWCFL at the beginning of season 2004/5.

With a record attendance of 495 against Halifax Town in 1996, and a listed capacity of 1000, the ground is one of those homely Lancashire stadia with its own idiosyncrasies.

The social club – open every night – is located outside the ground, but contains the chang-

Above: A single row of seats in the cover behind the clubhouse end goal

ing rooms. This means that to comply with NWCFL grading requirements, the club has the longest covered walkway from changing rooms to pitch of any of the grounds I've visited – it's more reminiscent of a circus than a football ground. It also has a large selection of different types of spectator accommodation.

The turnstiles are off the car park outside the social club, and are behind the goal line at the top end of a slightly sloping pitch. From the turnstile corner moving left along the goal line there are in turn; two rows of benches in the open, a three row small stand in front of the refreshment hut, a single row of covered seats immediately behind the goal, and an area of covered standing. Carrying on round the corner is a covered area with two rows of seats, and the sections nearest the corner are unique in having ordinary plastic chairs concreted into the ground.

Photo: Colin Peel

The only other covered accommodation is on the touchline opposite this, with one row of the high level tip-up seats that you more normally find in bus-shelters. The other half of the pitch has no cover on any of its three sides.

Founder members of the NWCFL, the club has twice been denied promotion – in 1995 and in 1998 – for ground grading reasons. The club sought planning permission to improve White Bank so that it would have been a focal point for the local community. Unfortunately the club had to abandon hopes of redeveloping. In 2008 they submitted plans for a new ground but the club now play at Atherton Collieries and are known as Oldham Borough.

Above right: A view along the clubhouse end goal line.
Above left: The chairs concreted in the side cover at the top end of the ground.
Above and below: Two views of the side cover at the top end of the ground.

Photo: Colin Peel

A panoramic view of the ground from the bottom end Photo: Colin Peel

Prescot Cables F.C.

Hope Street,
Prescot,
L34 5AW

Prescot Football Club was founded in 1884, and the first organised match was played against St Thomas` B from St Helens on 29th November on a field at Slackey Brow belonging to Prescot Cricket Club. A crowd of 3000 saw an FA Cup game played there against Crewe Alexandra in 1891/2. In July 1902 a dispute began between the football club and their landlords, with the result that the club lost their ground, could not fulfil its fixtures in the ensuing season, and folded.

Four years later a new ground with athletic and football facilities was opened at Hope Street, and a new club – Prescot Athletic – was formed. For most of the time since then the ground has been known as Hope Street (even though it is actually in Eden Street which is at the end of Hope Street). More re-cently it has been called Valerie Park after the deceased wife of a former chairman.

The club itself has also had a number of names since being created as Prescot Athletic, reverting simply to Prescot after WWI. They adopted the 'Cables' part of their name and changed their strip in 1928 as part of an early sponsorship arrangement with the principal local employer, who built a 1000 seat stand at the ground as part of the deal. The new black and amber strip was designed to match the paper with which the company wrapped their cable. In 1964 the club became Prescot Town for 16 years, and then re-adopted its current name in 1980.

The ground sits between rows of terraced housing and a rather upmarket residential area – almost as no-man's land between the two. Although the current capacity is given as 3,000, the record crowd is an amazing 8122 for a match against Ashton National in 1932, when the visiting supporters arrived in three special trains.

Entry is at one corner of the ground, and alongside the turnstiles there are vehicle access gates with a roadway leading to a minute car park behind the large main stand, built to replace the Cables sponsored stand which burnt down in 1960. This is one of the more imposing edifices amongst Lancashire non-league grounds, looking quite smart from a distance even with its liberal pigeon droppings. The seats appear to have been a job lot, with a wide range of colours installed randomly so that the effect is of a patchwork quilt. Unfortunately there are not quite enough seats to fill the space available. Under the stand is a well-set up social club and the changing rooms.

To the right of the entrance is a covered standing terrace, which extends from the corner flag to the near post, although it must at some stage have extended along the whole of that goal line, as the stumps of earlier supports are still in evidence. The currently covered area is parallel to the goal line, and the rest of that terracing is at an angle, getting closer to the corner flag but still leaving enough room for the pitch to be lengthened. The other two sides of the ground are uncovered, although there is an interesting banked and flat area alongside the touchline in the half furthest from the gate. There is also quite an impressive row of poplars behind the far goal, with a strange low fence which appeared to be made of pieces of advertising hoarding.

Although Hope Street is the home of Prescot Cables, I visited for a St Helens Town match – one of a couple played here in 2007. Apparently the owners of the ground at that time rented the ground not only to Prescot Cables itself, but to others including at various times Runcorn FC and Liverpool Ladies FC, as well as Prescot Panthers RLFC (formerly Highfield RLFC).

At the time of writing, the ground had recently been taken over by Triman Developments, and on 12th June 2008 the club signed a ten year lease for the use of the stadium. Announcements were made not only that the new AFC Liverpool will be ground sharing at Hope Street for their NWCFL home games in season 2008/9, but also that talks are being sought with Prescot Council about creating a new stadium within the town.

Above: The team in front of the old main stand in 1928. Photo: Dennis Bellairs
Below: The terrace at the covered end.

Inside the covered end terrace.

Radcliffe Borough F.C.

Stainton Park, Pilkington Road,
Radcliffe,
M26 3PE

I've been to Stainton Park many times – not least because Bury play their Reserve Team games there – and there always seem to be changes on the go. My visit very nearly coincided with the news that the club had been put up for sale by Chairman, Bernard Manning, Junior.

Founded in April 1949 by a gentleman called Jack Pickford, the club moved to its present ground in 1970, having previously played on two other grounds. The Non-League Club Directory shows a record crowd of 2495 but for a game played at Gigg Lane. Earlier editions show a crowd of 464 in 1997 against Haslingden during their brief spell in the NWCFL,

but Club Chief Executive Dave Murgatroyd tells me it was 1,468 against Caernarfon Town for the last game of the 1982/3 season. This all suggests that the indicated capacity of 3000 is unlikely ever to be reached. Nonetheless, the club has spent nearly half a million pounds on facilities in the last few years, and the ground now boasts first class community small-sided pitches and changing rooms.

Below: The cover along the car park side seen from the stand at the top of the ground.

Photo: Colin Peel

From the large car park you can either enter the Social Club or pass through the turnstiles. These give you access near the halfway line on one side of the pitch, which is a typical Lancashire end-to-end sloping playing surface, with a considerable fall from left to right as you enter. Along the top goal line runs a covered stand with seats. At one end this has a splendid glass-cased Press Box and executive box (now redundant after the erection of a sponsors` lounge as a conservatory-type extension to the Social Club).

The changing room block is in the top corner between the stand and the social club, outside which is open terracing. On the right of the turnstile is a run of covered standing accommodation. The dug outs are close together on the opposite side of the pitch, and there is no cover along that side, but terracing from which one can admire some rather smart gardens during any lull in play. At the bottom end of the slope is a short length of uncovered terracing.

Above: . A team photo from the early 70s showing an old section of cover and the works, long since demolished. Photo: Dave Murgatroyd, Radcliffe Borough FC.

Below: . The terracing at the bottom / Pilkington Road End. Photo: Colin Peel

Photo: Colin Peel

Ramsbottom United F.C.
Riverside Ground, Acrebottom, Ramsbottom,
BL0 0BS

The present Ramsbottom club was founded in 1966, playing on a pitch in Chatterton Park, just up the road in Stubbins. Now they play alongside Ramsbottom Cricket Club, but the 1893 OS Map shows a Cricket & Football Ground, with two pavilions, suggesting that each sport had its own. Within living memory the area was simply a cricket pitch until 1980.

To me, everything about the Riverside Ground is the antithesis of what is mercenary and grasping about so much of professional football. I was sitting on the park benches under the Jack Wolfenden stand when I got chatting to one of the guys who had been around two hours before kick-off, getting the ground ready for the game. It turned out to be Jack Wolfenden himself. It was an honour bestowed in recognition of the time he had given to the club over the years. The Ellis Timlin stand had also been named after another club stalwart, sadly now dead.

The magnificent wrought-iron gate at the entrance leads to the Ken Bridge Way – named after a former manager who died in post.

The club moved to the Riverside in 1980 when Henry Williams, one of the club's three founders, persuaded the cricket club to let them rent an unused corner of the ground. Unfortunately the position of the cricket pitch score box meant that the new football ground was rather wedge-shaped, but the rear steps did provide an ideally elevated view of the match action. Initially the players used the changing facilities in the cricket club pavilion. As things developed the football club managed to agree with the cricket committee that they would pay the £11,000 necessary for the demolition and relocation of the score box to give the footballers a bit more land, so that it was possible to lay out a true rectangle.

Photo: Mike Floate

Photo: Mike Floate

Photo: Mike Floate

Above, left: The two stands between the pitch and the river.
Above: The covered Jack Wolfenden stand.
Left: The club facilities by the entrance

the cricket club, the ground entrance nestles modestly in the corner of the cricket club car park, in the shadow of the back of the cricket pavilion. However, the decorative brick wall, the wrought-iron gate, and the general air of pride of appearance make it so different from many other North West Counties grounds.

The spectator path to the pitch leads down the side of the tea bar, which prides itself on selling hot drinks in proper china mugs. Towards the end of each game, someone circles the pitch with a tray, collecting the empties.

The old pavilions in 2002. Pic: Mike Floate

On the other side of the tea bar is a lawn, convenient for children to play, and separated by a fence from the changing rooms and the sponsors lounge, elevated at first floor level. A large clock completes the picture. The remainder of the east and all of the north sides of the ground are the ones most constrained by space, and simply have narrow strips of standing area between the pitch and the boundary fence. On the west side are two small stands – the older one with seats and the Ellis Timlin which is a covered standing area. The main covered area is the Jack Wolfenden stand along the south end of the pitch. Although principally a standing terrace, as mentioned it had a number of park benches for spectators on one of my visits.

When the club applied to join the NWCFL, they ended up with 16 weeks to enclose the ground fully, and to install their own changing and hospitality facilities. This was done, and today the collection of portakabins is the neatest and tidiest in the League. The ground sits below Holcombe Hill, with its famous Peel Tower, and is bounded on two sides by the cricket ground, on a third by the River Irwell, and on the fourth by the East Lancashire steam preservation railway.

Approached from the level crossing by Ramsbottom Railway Station down the road to

Rochdale Town F.C.

Castleton Sports Centre, Chadwick Lane, off Heywood Road, Castleton, OL11 3BY

Founded in 1924 as the team from St Gabriel's Catholic Church in Castleton, the club began its existence in the Rochdale Sunday League, playing in local parks. They were at Springfield Park from 1960 until they moved to their present home.

A prominent local businessman, Tom Butterworth, bought land and established a pitch for the club in 1979, and it was named Butterworth Park in his honour. Over the next few years the ground was progressively improved, with the clubhouse being built, and the club joined the NWCFL in 1990 as Castleton Gabriels.

Unfortunately financial turbulence set in when Tom Butterworth stopped contributing at the turn of the century and sold the land. There followed a period of great uncertainty and the club were within two days of being ejected from the League when Secretary Jim Picken and Oldham Town agreed a ground share. Consequently the club played the first few games of that season at the White Bank Stadium (see p. 38), worked on their own ground and moved back in the first week of November, 2004.

Eventually Butterworth Park was bought by Mayfield Amateur Rugby League club, on the back of the proceeds of selling their old ground for development, and the Gabriels became joint users of the facility. The ground is now renamed the Castleton Sports Centre, and there are very ambitious plans for the creation of a true community facility for rugby league, football and cricket.

The ground set-up is typical of so many clubs whose facilities have grown progressively over the years. Entry through the turnstiles brings you to the back of the main stand. To comply with ground grading requirements, the 2006/7 season saw the strengthening of the stand's structure, and a new hospitality suite/ sponsors lounge built on top.

To the right of this stand is a covered standing terrace, which stretches into and around the corner, and along the whole length of the goal line. Opposite is a covered terrace with two rows of seats, in front of which is the main walkway for spectators. To the left is an uncovered terracing of concrete steps which extends around the corner near the main stand. The two dug-outs are very long extensions on either side of the main stand.

In 2008 the club applied to the Lancashire FA to change their name to Rochdale Town as they had become extremely frustrated by the lack of support the club was receiving from Castleton and its residents. Every single business in the area had been approached, but not a single one had offered even the slightest assistance.

Initially the name change was rejected because of an objection from Rochdale FC, but after discussions between the clubs not only was the objection withdrawn, Rochdale also agreed to develop closer longer-term relationships.

Above: The uncovered concrete terrace.
Below: The terrace leads to an interesting angled corner section.

The covered seating opposite the main stand

Salford City F.C.

Moor Lane, Kersal,
Salford,
M7 3PZ

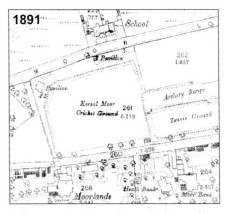

Moor Lane is certainly one of the more unusual grounds, in more ways than one. Whilst named after the busier road of the two between which it is located, the main entrance and the stand are on the Neville Road side of the ground. Driving along Moor Lane, it is only the top of the floodlight pylons, a non-descript sign and a solitary turnstile in a dilapidated concrete fence that give away the existence of a ground that once held a crowd of 3,000, but now has an official capacity of 1,400.

This area of land has an on-going sporting history which has been traced back as far as 1681 – for a variety of sports including archery, cricket, tennis, hockey, rugby, and finally football. The sporting history of the area is such that it merits a chapter in Simon Inglis` book, "Played in Manchester".

In the seventeenth century, what is now Neville Road was the finishing straight for Kersal Moor Racecourse, so what was originally a considerable slope down from Moor Lane must have provided a great natural grandstand. The race course can still be clearly seen on the 1848 Ordinance Survey map, but by 1891 the original circuit no longer existed in its entirety. A cricket ground had been created after major levelling work, with banking on three sides, but particularly at the Moor Lane side, where there were two pavilions. There was also a tennis 'ground' and an archery range. Neville Street was then Back Vine Street.

Photo: Colin Peel

Top: The side cover in 2008.
Above: The same cover in 1992/3. Photo courtesy of Atherton Laburnam Rovers.

Eventually the cricket pitch became the home of Manchester RFC who in 1978 passed on the lease to Salford Amateurs FC who played in the Manchester League. In 1980 they amalgamated with Anson Villa, who had been playing at Brantingham Road, but in the higher-regarded Cheshire County League. The merged club called themselves Salford FC, playing in the Cheshire League and so became founder members of the NWCFL in 1982. In 1990 they gained approval from the City of Salford to add City to their name. The 3000 crowd was against Whickham in the fourth round of the 1980/81 FA Vase.

The club boast a unique structure – a stand which is built of cast re-inforced concrete. Constructed in the 1930s by the rugby club, it shares the styling of Odeon cinemas of the era. The stand has a number of concrete steps, and the "seats" are simply planks screwed to these, other than in the Directors and Officials area where they have the luxury of plastic seats.

The most striking feature about the playing area is the amount of space between the pitch itself and the perimeter fencing. The pitch perimeter fencing is also concrete.

Opposite the main stand is a small covered three-bay standing enclosure with three concrete levels. At either end there is no cover, but plenty of space. At the end by the Neville Road entrance the area behind the goals is used for car parking, and the other for training and pre-match warm-ups.

Photo: Colin Peel

Trafford F.C.

Shawe View, Pennybridge Lane, Flixton, M41 5DL

Four former members of the Flixton FC committee formed the club as North Trafford FC in 1990 and have used the ground since then. Shawe View is one of those neat and well-ordered grounds, with the effect only being marginally spoilt by the agglomeration of tatty portable buildings which form the social club and changing rooms.

At the junction of two back lanes – the unsurfaced one being Shawe Road - the ground could be out in the wilds, but is only a few metres from Flixton Road, one of the major

Photo: Andy Dakin

routes through the area. There is a large car park outside, and the turnstiles are in one corner of the ground. On entering, the changing rooms and social club are to the left, and then further along that touchline there is a small seated stand with press box. The main walkway around the pitch is in front of those seats, which is a problem for those choosing to sit there. Behind the goal furthest from the entrance is the Sid Firmedow Stand – a covered standing area – named after a dedicated club member who had been Commercial Manager of the club until his death four years ago.

Top: The main stand looking towards the Sid Firmedow stand. Left: The stand was incomplete for many years. Photo: Andy Dakin Below: The same stand today.

Along the touchline opposite the changing rooms is the main seated accommodation, with private area for officials. In this stand, the walkway is within the covered area, but thankfully and unusually behind the seats. There is no cover behind the goal at the opposite end from the Sid Firmedow Stand.

The overall impression is of neatness and good order, with the steel work of all covered accommodation painted uniformly in dark green, and where there is no structure, the pitch is lined by tidy and well-maintained grass banks. Apparently 803 people attended a league game in season 1997/8 with local rivals Flixton.

The ground was originally created from a field, and it has seen a wide range of sides using it as home. Teams which have been based or simply played there over the years include Urmston Town (who played their two NWCFL seasons in the 1980`s at Shawe View), Altrincham Reserves, Manchester City A and B teams, Salford Rugby League club,

Above, left: The main seating area on the far side of the ground.
Above: The Sid Firmedow stand located behind the far goal.

and Trafford Borough Rugby League team – with whom Trafford shared the ground in their first season. After they obtained sole tenancy on a 30 year lease in 1991 they were able to undertake substantial improvements.

Trafford have had a slightly yo-yo existence of late. Having started in the Mid-Cheshire League, they joined the NWCFL two years later, changing their name to Trafford in 1994. The club gained promotion to the Unibond in 1997. Their stay was for six seasons, when they were relegated back to the NWCFL, but emerged as champions after a further five years and were promoted back into the Unibond in 2008.

Below, left: The inside of the main stand.
Below: The bank at the open end.

Abbey Hey F.C.
Abbey Stadium, Goredale Avenue, Gorton, M18 7HD

The home of Abbey Hey is a tribute to the committee that keep this club going – and improve the facilities – despite a never ending battle with vandalism. The committee's dedication was recently recognised by the Manchester FA who made long service awards in recognition of their work.

The club acquired the ground in 1984, the site being the former Abbey Hey Working Men's Club. The ground had not been a football pitch, but there was a bowling green in one corner – an area now used as a small sided training pitch. The pitch proper is some feet higher up than this.

The club house and changing rooms are between the pitch and an embankment, but provide no spectator cover. There is also a low covered structure along most of the opposite touchline. Interestingly, this has seats at either end, but none in the middle, and the roof comes down vertically at the front to provide additional weather protection over the standing area but not over the seated ends. This stand has a capacity of 300, but the record crowd is just 400 for a friendly in 1999 with an XI from the club's now near neighbours, Manchester City.

Irlam Steel F.C.

Liverpool Road,
Irlam,
M44 6AJ

Another works ground, formerly part of the sports facilities of the Irlam Steel Works, formerly Lancashire Steel. This huge works by the Manchester Ship Canal closed in 1980. There is not enough space for the cricket and football pitches to be used at the same time, so the football team only play mid-week games before mid-September. Early season Saturday games are played on a local park.

Work was done on the pitch in 2006 to reduce undulations, but unfortunately the groundwork cut into what was – before living memory – a refuse site. The club was stopped from using the pitch for a time until all the unearthed glass shards were cleared. Domed in the middle, the surface now looks good, although it is sometimes still checked before games.

The ground's unique feature is the old corrugated cover which extends the whole length of the far touchline.

The years after WW 2 saw the club playing in the Manchester League alongside sides such as Manchester United A and Manchester City A. Whilst the players weren't paid, there was an entry charge with a turnstile, a refreshment bar in the middle of the cover where a vintage wooden bench is now, and a rail along the front, the brackets for which still exist.

The team now play in the Lancashire and Cheshire Amateur League, and the old works Social Club is a members` club which owns the land outright. There have been discussions about restoring the old cover to its former glory but the remedial groundwork on the pitch cost £4,000, and the situation is complicated as the corrugated sheeting is asbestos, so specialist contractors will be required.

Photo: Colin Peel

Liverpool County FA

**Liverpool Soccer Centre,
Walton Hall Park,
Liverpool, L4 9XP**

Based at the Walton Hall Park sports complex, the Liverpool County FA have their offices within the sports centre itself, and two County pitches on the site. Both pitches are magnificent, receiving particular devotion from the centre's ground staff.

The main pitch shows no sign of the 40 games played there each season. With its own cover for standing spectators, fully railed, with a sprinkler system and eight pylon floodlighting system, it is made available for local cup finals and other high profile matches.

Plans for further development include the provision of an Astroturf strip along each touchline for the Linesmen (sorry, referees` assistants.), for seating, and for a turnstile and improved fencing.

Alongside the County FA pitch is its twin, the Schools pitch, which hosts about 60 games each season. Once again a credit to the ground staff, the schools pitch is a virtual duplicate, featuring a stand and dugouts which are identical to the ones on the County pitch. The only difference is that the schools pitch is marginally smaller – approximately 6 yards narrower and just over 2 yards shorter.

The rear of the main stand on the far side of the schools pitch.

Maghull F.C.
Old Hall Field,
Hall Lane, Maghull,
L31 3DY

Founded in 1921, the club played on a pitch at Deyes Lane which had its own pavilion/stand but is now under St Andrew's School. In the 1950`s they moved to their present ground at Hall Lane. The club has played in the I-Zingari Alliance, the I-Zingari League, the Liverpool County Combination, and joined the Lancashire Combination in 1972.

They then moved to the Cheshire County League in 1978 and became founder members of the NWCFL in 1982. Division Two Champions in 1993, they were not promoted as their ground did not meet the grading standards for the higher division. In fact, as the grading standards progressively got tighter, the club left the NWCFL in 1999 since they did not have covered accommodation for 500. Rather than joining one of the Liverpool Leagues, they entered the West Cheshire League.

The Old Hall Playing Fields are owned by Maghull Town Council, and are approached down the leafy Tommy Gent Way (named after an old gentleman who once lived in the cottage by the side of it, not some famous local sportsman). This leads to an enormous car park, in front of which is a great open space which is more than adequate for both football and cricket pitches with no overlap as in so many other shared grounds. Trees surround the area which is overlooked by the tower of the local church. According to the notice by the entrance, the Playing Fields are the home of the Maghull Football and Cricket Club, but there are two distinct club houses at opposite sides of the field. The football changing rooms and clubhouse were built after a fire in 1991 destroyed the previous facilities.

Although without floodlights, the football pitch is permanently railed on all four sides, and the dugouts are provided with shutters against vandals and courting couples. The football club clubhouse has a covered terrace from which the game can be watched if the weather is bad, and there is a railed player walkway from the changing rooms to the pitch.

The Manchester League

Atherton Town F.C.
Howe Bridge, Atherton, M46 0QQ

The junior of the Atherton named Saturday teams has the flattest pitch. Situated behind a sports complex and Atherton CC, the pitch is separate from the changing facilities which are effectively on the cricket club car park.

Following the path to the pitch, past the container which acts as the refreshment hut, one passes through a gate into a concrete fenced arena with a well-maintained pitch, recently renewed advertising hoardings, dug-outs, and spectator hard standing but currently nothing else in the way of spectator facilities.

Above: Atherton Town F.C.

Below: The view from the pavilion at Breightmet United F.C.

Breightmet United F.C.
Moss Park, Back Bury Road, Bolton BL2 6QU

This easterly suburb of Bolton has one of the longest established non-league teams in Lancashire. There is some debate about the actual date of the club's foundation, but the majority opinion is 1888. One of the club's yearbooks from that era is in the National Football Museum in Preston.

Playing at Moss Park from at least the 1920s they bought the land from a local farmer for £1,500 in the 1950s. Their present clubhouse was built in 1993, but its predecessor had been used as the HQ for the local Home Guard unit during WWII.

With a typical Lancashire address, the ground is down a little side road off a major arterial road in Bolton. A grant of £18,000 to help with fencing has reduced vandalism.

The ground itself is entered through large gates, and the clubhouse and changing rooms are on the left. The pitch is further on with an area of raised terracing outside the clubhouse alongside a bank up to an artificial 5-a-side pitch.

Breightmet United F.C.

Breightmet United F.C.

East Manchester F.C.
Wright Robinson College,
Gorton, M18 8RL

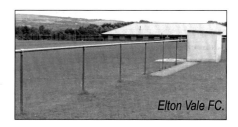
Elton Vale FC.

Formed as the Ferranti Engineering Factory team in 1960, they have subsequently been ICT, and then ICL before adopting their present name in 1983. Mount Road (Levenshulme, M19 3ET) is described on their website as their "old stomping ground", but in between times they have played at Kirkmanshulme Lane and when forced to leave there, at Droylsden`s ground. Mount Road was the Greater Manchester Transport sports ground and formerly had a simple cover, now gone. For season 2008/9 the club moved to Wright Robinson College to play on the artificial pitch. The limited facilites did not merit including a photo in this book.

Gregorians F.C.
Platt Lane, Manchester City Academy,
Yew Tree Road, Fallowfield, M14 7UU

Formed in 1959 as the club for the old boys of St Gregory's Grammar School – long gone – their first and reserve teams now play on the third generation artificial pitch at Manchester City`s Platt Lane complex, for which they pay the princely annual sum of about £11,000 for use every Saturday. Currently on a five year contract there, the club say that their aim is to apply to join the NWCFL, whose views on such pitches have moved on since rejecting Prescot BI's request to use one in 1985 (see p. 87). The limited photographic opportunities at this ground did not merit including a photo.

Elton Vale F.C.
Elton Vale, Elton Vale Road, Bury, BL8 2RZ

From the teams they have played in pre-season friendlies in recent years this appears to be an ambitious club. A visit to their facilities supports that view – they are superb, in a fantastic setting.

Elton Vale are a long-established sports club - and very lucky. They played for many years on a pitch on Bolton Road, shared with the club's cricket team, but not large enough for them both to be able to play at the same time. Their landlord was a local church which decided to sell the ground for housing development – here is where the good fortune comes in - but only on the proviso that the developer built the sports club a new facility.

As a result, in 1999 they moved onto a new site in a rural setting (well, as rural as it gets in Bury), with room for two totally separate pitches, and a clubhouse and changing rooms in between.

In terms of ambition, however, the club is more modest than it would appear, and they are very conscious that the costs of progressing to Step 6 are – at present – beyond their means.

Elton Vale FC.

Heywood St James F.C.
Phoenix Park, Shepherd St, OL10 1JW

The ground features on the 1875 OS map. It is shown as a football ground on the 1893 map, but as an "Athletic Ground" in 1910, 1929, 1932 and 1937. The layout on some of these suggests that it was not used for football for some of this time. There is also uncertainty over which club actually played there – Heywood F.C., West End, Central or Olympic, but not Heywood United who played most of their games at Bamford Road. The club believe it was Heywood Central's ground.

It is now the home of Heywood St James who were formed in at least 1882, their first recorded game being a 1-2 loss to Birtle in that year. For most of their early years they also played on Bamford Road, but took over their present pitch in 1933 and returned it to football – possibly the reason for 'Phoenix' Park? There was a wooden stand in existence at the end of WWII, but it had disappeared by the early 1950s.

There are plans to redevelop the club's buildings which sit on an elevated position at one end of the pitch. The club have floodlights donated by Manchester United as Duncan Edwards` first game for Man Utd Colts had been against Heywood St James on 23rd August 1952.

Heywood St James F.C. Pic: John Rhodes

Heywood St James F.C.

Hindsford A.F.C.
Squires Lane, Tyldesley, M29 8JF

The Hindsford pitch is rented from a member of the aristocracy, and is down a lengthy and increasingly up-market cul-de-sac in Tyldesley – all of which belies the origins of the club. Hindsford was founded by a group of miners in 1926 during the miners` strike.

They first played at the wonderfully named Print Shop Lane, moving a stone's throw to their present location in approximately 1961, after which the old ground had a school built upon it.

They took over a field, and converted it to a football pitch which slopes quite significantly from one goal to the other. Members of the Lancashire Combination in the early 1950`s, they have played in the Manchester League since 1998, and gained promotion to the Premier Division in 2005.

Over the last five years the club has spent in excess of £40,000 on developing/improving the clubhouse, pitch, drainage, car park, fencing and standing areas. The clubhouse is well-protected against vandals, and boasts a small area of covered standing at the half-way line. With very large areas of hard standing for parking, and plenty of touchline advertising, the whole set-up is well maintained and smart.

Future plans include extending and upgrading the changing rooms and increasing the cover for spectators, but currently without any ambitions to move from the Manchester League.

Hindsford A.F.C.

Hollinwood CC F.C.
Lime Lane, Roman Road, Hollinwood OL8 3TB
Chapel Road, Grammar School Rd, OL8 4QY

Named after a cricket club, their first and second teams have moved away from the cricket club, now playing on a third generation artificial pitch at Chapel Road, an Oldham municipal centre.

The Cricket Club dates back to 1877, and has had an associated football club for much of this time, originally taking over a football pitch, buying the football club's tent, pay box, and other fittings. The present Lime Lane ground was bought for £750 in 1914, but the current football club only started in the 1950`s as a Sunday side. It progressed through to the Manchester League in the early 1970`s. For a time the League felt the Lime Lane ground was unfit, but with an FA grant the club overhauled the playing area. In typical Manchester League fashion, the ground is not quite big enough for both sports to have independent playing areas, so the football pitch is only railed on three sides.

Situated between a cemetery and the M60, the ground now only hosts the club's third team, but their website says it "will remain as our real home".

Leigh Athletic F.C.
Leigh Sports Village, Turner Way, WN7 4JY

The club was formed as Old Leighans in 1958 and three years later began an association which continues today by moving to a pitch at the Holden Road athletics track – home of Leigh Harriers. They changed their name to Leigh Amateurs in 1965 and joined the Manchester League in 2000.

In February 2008 the club moved to the pitch in the middle of the new Leigh Harriers Athletics Stadium. The building backing on to the stand is the athletic club's headquarters, with multiple changing rooms and with an 80 metre warming up track on the upper floor, under the roof, but open at the sides.

As with all football clubs playing in the middle of an athletics stadium, the major problem is spectator involvement. The facilities are great, but there is an 8 lane track and a long-jump run-up between the spectator facilities and the pitch.

Leigh Athletic rent the pitch and use of the changing rooms, and plan on settling in for two or three seasons before considering whether or not to aspire to the NWCFL.

Above: The Lime Road ground. Below: The artificial pitch at Chapel Road.

Pennington F.C.
Jubilee Park, Leigh Road, Atherton, M46 0SE

The club was founded in 1970, as a junior club in Pennington, which is a suburb of Leigh. They used to play on a park pitch there, but could not afford to buy land or take out a lease in that area.

Consequently they got a lease on their present ground in Atherton from Wigan Borough Council in 1981, taking over what had formerly been a 'ruck' – the local name for a slag heap. It had been levelled but this still explains why the sylvan lane leading to the ground from Leigh Road rises quite steeply at the pitch end. They effectively started from scratch, and over the years have fenced the area, installed new field drainage, and added over 100 tons of topsoil. Now that trees have grown around the land, the truly rural appearance belies its origins.

Initially accommodation at Jubilee Park was in a Kenkast structure that had previously been the Nurses Home at Crewe Memorial Hospital. Sadly this burnt down in February 1996 and has since been replaced by a smaller brick changing room structure.

Currently the club is in the process of planning to build a new clubhouse and to take over adjacent land to create junior pitches.

Pennington F.C.

Pennington F.C.

Prestwich Heys A.F.C.
Sandgate, Sandgate Lane, Whitefield, M456WG

The club moved to Sandgate from Grimshaws (see p. 82) in 1991. Parallel with the M60 and in the shadow of some of the largest national grid pylons (bigger than Flixton but fewer), the site has potential for development.

The Sandgate ground gives Heys the space to develop and there is considerable ambition within the club to take advantage of this potential. There are two turnstiles by the entrance, currently uncovered, and a base has already been laid for the erection of a prefabricated stand. Floodlights have been purchased but the major hitch to further progress had been obtaining planning permission to erect the pylons. The committee finally obtained permission in November 2007 to erect new buildings, fencing, extend the car park and erect floodlights. The club are now working on funding for the project with a view to making an application to rejoin the NWCFL in the next two years.

Prestwich Heys A.F.C.

Prestwich Heys A.F.C.

Prestwich Heys A.F.C.

Rochdale Sacred Heart F.C.
Fox Park, Belfield Mill Lane, OL16 2UB

Founded in 1955 to play in the Rochdale Sunday Schools League, the club moved to the South East Lancashire League and then in 1982 to the Manchester League, playing all the while on park pitches. However, in 1985 they merged with Robinson Football and Cricket Club which had its own ground at Fox Park. The cricket team continued in its own right, and the two football teams merged as RSH85, reverting to the original Sacred Heart name in 1988. There is almost but not quite enough space at Fox Park for the two sports to have totally separate playing areas, so Fox Park is another pitch railed on three sides.

In 2001 new drains were installed and levelling work carried out on the playing area.

Royton Town F.C.
Crompton CC, Christine Street, Shaw, OL2 7SF

Another ex-company team – the club was founded as the Stotts Benham works side in 1980, becoming Royton Town in 1985. Previously playing on a pitch at Monarch Mill, the owner wanted to develop the site. As a result they moved to Crompton Cricket Club in 2000 to an attractive and separate playing area. However, there is little scope for further development here and the club are searching for a home that would give them more opportunity.

Royton F.C.

Royton F.C.

Rochdale Sacred Heart F.C.

Royton F.C.

Springhead F.C.
Ashfield Cres. Springhead, Oldham, OL4 4NX

Formed as Lees Amateurs in 1922, the club have played on their present ground since that time. The result of a lot of hard work in the past to get a reasonably level playing surface, one touchline is very much carved out of the bank, and there is a gravel drain along that touchline to deal with the water that comes down from higher up – the head of the spring, presumably.

Photo: Rob Turley

Top: The old bowls pavilion. Above: The derelict ground after East Chorlton folded.

Originally the land had been an integral part of the Chorltonville Estate, a garden suburb of Arts and Crafts houses built before WWI to rent to 'skilled artisans', and now the most upmarket part of Chorlton. Brochures of the time describe how, "5½ acres of land has been set apart for Recreation Grounds. Five Tennis Courts and a large bowling green have been laid. A delightful and picturesque Pavilion has been erected."

Residents were not so enthusiastic about the facilities as hoped, and after WWII the land was sold off. The bowling green was sold to become a back garden, and the pavilion, tennis courts and children's area were bought by St Bede`s OB Rugby Club in 1957. They created a pitch and used the pavilion as clubhouse and changing rooms. In the 1960s the single pitch had become inadequate, and it was sold it to East Chorlton F.C.

West Didsbury & Chorlton F.C.
Brookburn Road, Chorltonville, M21 8EH

Known as Wests, the club was founded in 1908 as Christ Church A.F.C. They became West Didsbury in season 1920/21 when they joined the Lancashire & Cheshire League. Originally playing on a field by the church on Darley Avenue, from 1914 they used Christie Fields on the opposite side of Princess Parkway. The club were given notice to leave in the 1990s, and the land is now under office blocks. For a few years the club was homeless until it moved to its current home, which is well hidden down a sylvan lane in the Chorltonville Conservation Area.

East Chorlton were based there for around 30 years before they folded, and the ground was left unused. During their nomadic period Wests had suggested a merger with East Chorlton and eventually bought the land. Now a new clubhouse has been built, the pitch is superb, and the whole set-up is immaculate. The clubhouse has a large porch which can be used as covered standing spectator accommodation during bad weather. The ground was ready for use for the 1997/8 season.

Since then there has been an ongoing programme of improvements, with new drainage, laser-levelling of the pitch and spectator hardstanding.

Chorlton was added to the original club name in 2003 as part of a drive to increase local involvement, and the first game under the new name was a friendly with Altrincham which attracted a crowd of almost 200. After 86 years' membership the club left the Lancashire & Cheshire League, joining the Manchester League for season 2006/7.

West Didsbury & Chorlton F.C.

Whitworth Valley F.C.
Rawstron Street, Whitworth, OL12 8BA

They must have had to look long and hard to find a patch of land anything like level in Whitworth. It truly is a valley, with road access only up or down it – certainly not across. Prepared for a game at the time of our visit, the ground was spick and span, and the grass newly mown, even though the club's mower had been stolen the previous week.

Now sandwiched between two residential roads, the 1893 OS Map shows the area as "Whitworth Football & Cricket Ground" and what is now Crown Park Way South to the west of the ground was the Facit Branch of the Lancashire and Yorkshire Railway. Around the ground was what appears to be a running track.

The odd-shaped bowling green in the corner is now square, and the North end of the ground has been lost. Now the pitch is railed on three sides, but the touchline on the opposite side from the changing rooms gives straight onto bushes and then the ground's external railings. There is a variable slope from side to side, with the changing room corner as the highpoint of the pitch. There is a noticeable embankment down to the road along much of the lower touchline.

Behind the far goal are the remnants of what was once covered standing accommodation – now lacking a roof. There is one small stand next to the changing rooms, although it resembles an old-fashioned park shelter rather than a football stand. It appears to be the evening haunt of the local young people, sporting a display of graffiti. I was particularly taken with the striped plastic chairs in the dugouts.

Originally one of the founding members of the North West Counties Division Three, but with no floodlights and insufficient covered accommodation to meet grading requirements, Whitworth Valley now play in the Manchester League. The club rent the ground from Whitworth Council, and before they started to use it, the area was apparently still a running track. Senior members of the club reckon that the record attendance was about 400 in approximately 1971 for the first match of the season which was a game against local rivals Bacup Borough. I was unable to discover when the present club was founded and when it first played at Rawstron Street.

Whitworth Valley F.C.

Whitworth Valley F.C.

Wythenshawe Amateurs F.C.
Wythenshawe Cricket Club, 78 Longley Lane, Northenden M22 4JH

The Amateurs were founded in 1946 as Wythenshawe Lads Club, becoming Wythenshawe Amateurs in 1951 as the lads got older and into open-age football.

Currently their ground is part of the Wythenshawe Club, where they share the space with Wythenshawe CC, a relationship that has become increasingly complex as the overlapping cricket and football pitches hinder eachothers' development. However they do have dug-outs and a pitch railing, together with the use of an excellent clubhouse/changing room complex.

The club gained outline planning permission three years ago to develop a 3,000 capacity stadium to NWCFL standards in Hollyhedge Park, a public park in Wythenshawe, and work was due to begin in July 2008.

Wythenshawe Amateurs F.C.

Walshaw Sports Club F.C.
Sycamore Road, Tottington, BL8 3EH

Members of the Manchester League since 2005, Walshaw has had a football team "of one kind or another" (to quote the club`s website) since the 1890`s, playing on a variety of pitches. In 1965 the football team and village cricket team merged to form Walshaw Sports Club, securing a long lease on Sycamore Road.

Since then they have worked to develop the playing surfaces and facilities, but there is not enough room for two separate pitches. Walshaw only have railing at one side. The lack of facilities have meant I have not included a photo of this ground.

Wythenshawe Town F.C.
Ericstan Park, Timpson Road, Baguley, M23 9NT

Formed as North Withington F.C. in 1946, with a park ground on Princess Road, the club was renamed Wythenshawe Town in 1987.

Unfortunately our enquiries with the club failed to discover when they moved to their current ground, and whether or not they created it from scratch. The ground was named Ericstan Park as a tribute to two of the club's early prime movers, Eric Reynard and Stan Orme.

With their senior team now playing in the Manchester League, and 13 teams in total, the club has a main pitch and a junior pitch next door.

The main pitch is well-concealed behind a splendid row of trees off one of the busiest roads in Manchester, entry being gained at the opposite end through a pair of wrought iron gates off a road behind the supermarket.

The clubhouse still bears the sign of Manchester City Ladies who used to play there, but the pitch is now shared with Altrincham's Academy who use it on Sundays.

Wythenshawe Town F.C.

Wythenshawe Town F.C.

With railings around three sides, and dug-outs on opposite touchlines, there is a small stand alongside the home dugout, and a concrete based scaffold framework at the side of the away one – presumably awaiting a permanent roof. The club-house is by the entrance, and has a range of outside tables from which the game may be watched in good weather, and a porch to provide shelter in less clement conditions.

Wythenshawe Town F.C.

Wythenshawe Town F.C.

Wythenshawe Town F.C.

Liverpool Ramblers F.C.
Moor Lane, Thornton, L23 4TN

The club was formed in 1882, when a group of ex-pupils from Eton and Harrow found that many of the existing Liverpool clubs were for the old boys of Liverpool schools, and so joined together to create a team themselves. Some of the initial members had played for the first Bootle club under the auspices of the Deacon of St Johns Church, but left when he relocated away from the area. Surprisingly the club are members of the Lancashire rather than the Liverpool FA.

The team have never joined a league but tour regularly and enter certain competitions. For a long time they played on the Northern Cricket Club, but recently acquired their own pitches in Thornton, building a clubhouse overlooking the main pitch.

Liverpool Ramblers F.C.

The Liverpool County Premier League

Old Xaverians F.C.
St Francis Xaviers College, Beconsfield Road, L25 6EG

Seems quite logical that the Old Xaverians should play on a pitch at the Xaverian College, but it really has not always been thus. The club was founded in 1892, as the winter section of the Old Xaverian Cricket Club, and they played at Newsham Park. Over the next ninety years they had a further six grounds across Merseyside before taking up residence at the alma mater in 1983.

Approaching their 120th anniversary, the club have an interesting history, including a four-match tour of Holland in 1902 at the invitation of the Dutch FA.

Their pitch is in a very pleasant almost rural setting at the back of the school grounds, with changing in an old house. The pitch has been railed, but the posts were not inserted far enough, so do not currently provide an effective or continuous barrier.

ROMA F.C.
Scargreen, Scargreen Avenue, Norris Green, L11 3DA

Finding a team called ROMA in the middle of Liverpool, you may imagine that someone is trying to live the continental dream. Sorry to disappoint you, but ROMA is an acronym for the Royal Oak on Muirhead Avenue. Formed as Mentmore FC in 1968, the name was changed in the 70s when the club joined the I-Zingari Alliance.

The club played on a number of grounds including the Kirkby Stadium from the end of the 1990`s. They shared the ground with Bootle for one season; the different ground grading standards of the different leagues are reflected in the fact that the NWCFL excluded Bootle because of the problems with Kirkby, but Roma played there until 2007.

When it was closed and demolished a new centre was built, but without a football pitch. Roma secured the lease of their current pitch in Norris Green at what is now known as Scargreen. They moved in at the beginning of season 2007/8 after the council spent £1 million, giving them superb new changing rooms and what they believe to be currently the best playing surface in the Liverpool County FA Premier League - an oasis in the middle of a large housing estate.

South Sefton Borough F.C.
Mill Dam Field, Behind the Punch Bowl, Lunt Road, Sefton Village, L29 7WA

This is the most idyllic location of any of the pitches in the Liverpool County Premier Division – as well as being one of the oldest. Approached down a lane between The Punchbowl and Sefton church, a small sign on a fence is the only indication that the ground is near. Follow a footpath separated from The Punchbowl's garden by a row of conifers by piles of flagstones stored for future hard standing. The changing block is on the left; the pitch is railed and dugouts have recently been built.

South Sefton Borough were founded in 2001, and played at a number of locations. Sefton & District FC agreed to share their Mill Dam Field pitch, and they began season 2006/7 as joint occupants, but sadly Sefton & District folded during that season.

They had been formed in 1919 as Birches United, after Mr Alfred Birch, their Chairman and owner of Sefton Corn Mills who let them use his field free of charge. Initially the players changed in stables, with a bucket as washing facilities, but then built a pavilion on Brickwall Lane which survived until the mid-1980's when new changing rooms were built.

South Sefton Borough's committee of five have worked hard to develop and improve the pitch and facilities they inherited.

South Sefton Borough F.C.

During the 2007 close season they lengthened the pitch, put the rail all round, and worked hard to get everything to its present spruce state. Improvements are planned to the changing rooms and for spectator hard standing.

Speke F.C.
Dunlops, Speke Hall Avenue, L21 1XA

Speke's current ground is just off the approach to Liverpool Airport, just outside the car park perimeter fencing. It is easily passed without notice, and if you do see it, you tend to hurry on because it looks like something from the worst of Beirut. This is sad, because there is a great history here. Before WWII the club and ground belonged to Rootes whose factory was nearby. After the war, it was taken over by Dunlop whose factory was across the road – then named Dunlop Road. The old road sign features at the entrance to the changing rooms.

In those far off glory days the sports complex had an active social club, and a full-time groundsman who looked after tennis courts, bowling green, rugby pitch, two football pitches, and an area for testing the performance of Dunlop golf balls. Jim Davies, the legendary manager/secretary of Waterloo Dock describes those pitches as being at that time, "One of the best grounds in Liverpool".

South Sefton Borough F.C.

Speke F.C.

Speke FC was founded as Speke Pegasus (after the Pegasus pub) in 1971, and amalgamated with the Dunlop football club in 1977, taking over the ground that is still known as "Dunlops". The football club is now separate from the social club, although their buildings adjoin. The ground belongs to the owners of Liverpool Airport, and is marked for use for future expansion. The social club will be given a pub called The Fox which is just outside the current ground, and Speke will move to a pitch at the now-demolished Central Avenue School. Unfortunately Speke do not know when that will be, and so the facilities are run down. Even though they were only opened in 1992 the changing rooms are what secretary Bill Locke describes as leaking and rat-infested. The balcony of the pavilion/changing rooms would once have been an ideal spot to watch games in bad weather, but ex-WD steel barricading has had to be fitted for security.

Even so, the pitch is in remarkably fine condition – whilst it still exists.

Waterloo Dock F.C
Dockers Club, Townsend Lane, Liverpool, L13 9DY

Formed in 1963 as Victoria, with a team entered in the Liverpool Business Houses League, they changed their name to Waterloo Dock after the first two years. At that time there were twelve dock teams playing under the auspices of the Merseyside Dockworkers Sports and Social Organisation, but of these only two Saturday teams remain – Waterloo Dock and great local rivals, Bootle.

In 1970 the team moved into the Liverpool County Combination. They play at the Dockers Club in Edinburgh Park, which used to belong to the National Dock Labour Board. The enormous fortress-like social club fronts the road, and behind it there are three pitches. NELTC groundshare here, and other clubs have been tenants over the years, including Bootle for one season whilst they were homeless after the closure of Kirkby.

On-going success has led the club to look into moving up from Step Seven, and they are currently in talks with a developer over plans to cede some of the land in exchange for building a stadium and installing lights so that application can be made to join the NWCFL.

Speke F.C.

Waterloo Dock F.C.

Speke F.C.

Waterloo Dock F.C.

Additional Liverpool League clubs

These clubs have simple facilities not warranting a photo but are included to complete the details of the League.

Birchfield F.C.
Edge Hill University, Ormskirk, L39 4QP

Founded in 1989, Birchfield have grown out of Birchfield Infant School. As the lads have got older they now play their home games at Sporting Edge, the Edge Hill University's 25 acre sports complex.

BRNESC
Railway Club, Melling Road, Aintree, L9 0LQ

Pronounced as Brr-Nesk, this club is in the same heritage line as Horwich RMI, Newton Heath Loco and Manchester United. The club was originally Aintree Loco, founded in 1905. They moved to their present ground at the junction of Seeds Lane and the famous (to Grand National fans, anyway) Melling Road in 1920. Initially their changing facilities were in an old railway carriage.

In 1942, the pitch was taken over for military purposes, and used by the Americans as a storage depot for tank spares. After hostilities ceased, the Americans re-laid the pitch, installing new drainage before handing it back to the footballers in 1950

Originally surrounded by fencing made of old railway sleepers on end, and in the shadow of a railway embankment. When the railways were nationalised after WW II, the club changed its name to British Rail North End Social Club.

For many years the ground was shared with cricket, but now only football is now played. There are two pitches, the larger being used for Saturday football and the smaller for Sunday. The heritage remains in the quality of the playing surface – a tribute to American drainage – and an enormous cricket roller.

Collegiate Old Boys F.C.
Alder Sports Club, Alder Road, West Derby, L12 2BA

Founded in 1909 for the old boys of Liverpool Collegiate School the club have played on many grounds. For the last few seasons have been using a pitch at Holly Lodge Girls School. They now ground share with Alder F.C.

East Villa F.C.
Long Lane, MYA Jeffreys Humble, Fazakerley, L9 9AQ

Founded in 1959, the club played on a private pitch known as Jack Sharps in Fazackerley. The "East" is thought to originate from Muirhead Avenue East, the area from which they originated. For 30 years East Villa have played on the prime pitch on the Long Lane sports ground. Their pitch was once an athletics club, and is surrounded by the remains of a running track with a fence of concrete posts and slabs, but sadly most of the slabs have long since disappeared. East Villa will be moving for season 2008/9 to the Litherland Park Sports Centre.

NELTEC

Formed in 1961 for the old boys of Walton Technical School, the club has been known as NETC before becoming North East Liverpool Technical College. They play at the Edinburgh Park Dockers Club.

Lucas Sports F.C.
William Collins Playing Field, Commercial Rd, L5 7QY

Originally part of the Sports and Social Club of the Lucas Aerospace factory, the club was formed in 1960, and played on the company's sports ground at Edenhurst Avenue, Huyton. In 1982 the company decided that they could no longer maintain the sports facilities and the pavilion was soon vandalised. The football team were forced to play on a council pitch for three or four seasons.

An agreement was reached for a ground share between Old Holts and Lucas Sports but unfortunately this arrangement did not last long into the new century and the club moved out in 2002. They played for two seasons in Allerton, moving to their present pitch in 2006.

Red Rum F.C.
Croxteth School, Parkstile Lane, L11 0BD

They have played here since forming in 1984.

South Liverpool F.C.
Jericho Lane, Liverpool L17 5AR

When the limited company running the club folded in 1991 the old club committee carried on with the running of the team. For season 1992/3 they merged with Cheshire Lines, playing in the Liverpool County Combination as Cheshire Lines South Liverpool on the Cheshire Lines pitch, but then demerged after the one season.

South are now playing in the Liverpool County FA Premier Division on a park pitch in Aigburth, just a few miles from their original home, but hope to get a longer lease and develop the facilities.

St Aloysius F.C.
King George V Playing Fields, Longview Lane, L36 7UN

Founded in 1934, the club have been playing on a pitch at the King George V playing fields in Huyton for six years.

Lost Football Grounds and Stadia
Fallowfield Stadium, Manchester

Two FA Cup Finals have been played in Manchester. In 1915 at Old Trafford, and in 1893 it was played at Fallowfield Athletic Grounds.

The FA had found themselves without a home for the final in 1893 as Kennington Oval had become too small. It is still a mystery why the FA did not decide the game should be played at the Crystal Palace Grounds in London but in their wisdom they settled on this venue.

The Cup Final record crowd prior to 1893 was 32,500. The Fallowfield arena was variously described as having 'a capacity of 15,000', or being 'able to hold no more than 25,000' and was obviously far too small yet this seemed to have been of little importance. The game was played on 25th March, and the official attendance was supposedly 45,067, but a crowd estimated at 60,000 had managed to get into the ground.

The pavilion in the south-east corner

It is a great tribute to the good nature of those attending that there were no serious injuries, despite the vast majority being unable to see anything. Spectators were continually encroaching the touchlines, such that the two teams` wingers were left as virtual spectators, with high balls being pumped down the middle. After a goalless first half, Wolves scored in very controversial circumstances, when an Everton player had the ball nicked off his feet by a spectator as he was about to clear it, and it ended up with the Wolves captain who lobbed the keeper from distance. Everton demanded that the game be replayed, but it was deemed that the result should stand as Everton had not complained until after they lost.

The 1893 Cup Final crowd at Fallowfield. Photo: Manchester Central Library

The FA did not learn the lesson from the problems, and used Fallowfield as an FA Cup Semi-Final venue in 1899. Sheffield United played Liverpool, and the game had to be abandoned because of a crush in the crowd.

The Athletic Grounds were opened in May 1892 by Manchester Athletics Club who had been forced to move from their home next to Old Trafford Cricket Ground. It was also used occasionally for rugby union, and the last England-Scotland international played outside London took place there in 1897. Subsequently it became a cycling stadium with a banked track, owned for a time by the legendary cyclist Reg Harris, and named after him.

Below: By 1907 a stand has been built on the south side of the pitch. The road to the east of Fallowfield in the map below is now Whitworth Lane.

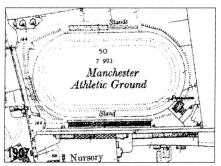

It was bought by Manchester University in the 1960`s, incorporated into their sports facilities, and then demolished in 1994 to become the site for the Richmond Park Halls of Residence, on the east side of Whitworth Lane.

The venue was clearly not fit for hosting an FA Cup final but does exemplify that the authorities then were quite capable of ignoring the interests of paying spectators.

Photo: Jon Weaver

Photo: Jon Weaver

Above: The photos were taken in 1992 from the southeast corner of the stadium.
Below: Fallowfield looking east in 1955.

Photo: Manchester Central Library

South Liverpool F.C.
Holly Park

The generally accepted story is that South Liverpool, once arguably the leading Merseyside non-League team, were driven from their Holly Park home in Garston by constant vandalism, and that after years of battling they gave up the ghost and went ground sharing with Bootle.

A South Liverpool club was formed in 1898 but disbanded in 1921 when its then ground was requisitioned, and it reformed as New Brighton FC across the river. A new South Liverpool was formed in 1935, with a home at Holly Farm, the site of a former dairy business. A stadium was built funded by public donations, with a capacity of 15,000 and a clubhouse on site.

Below: The superb old main stand had seen better days when photographed in 1978. Both photos: Bob Lilliman

After WWII it is believed that the club became the first in the world to have permanent floodlights, which were inaugurated on 28th September 1949 with a match against a Nigerian XI. A crowd of 13,000 saw a 2-2 draw, in which the traditional caseys were painted white, and commentator on the day was Kenneth Wolstenholme. Some sources claim this to have been the first modern floodlit game in Britain, but the first ever is said to belong to Darwen`s Barley Bank, with a game played under temporary lights on 28th October 1878 marginally predating South Liverpool.

Below: The covered terrace beside the West Coast line into Liverpool Lime Street in 1978.

Having the lights, South Liverpool were able to play on Friday night to avoid direct competition with the major Football League teams in the area, and in 1968 they became founder members of the Northern Premier League. The club applied unsuccessfully for election to the Football League on ten occasions.

The club suffered major fire damage in 1976, in 1984, and again in 1989. The stand was rebuilt after the 1984 fire, but the last destroyed the clubhouse and made the ground unsafe. Further vandalism was quoted as the reason for the club closing the ground in 1990.

South played the 1990/91 season at Bootle's Bucks Park. South Liverpool was a limited company, and it had just been taken over by a new owner. The previous administration had put up with the vandalism for many years, but the new owner prefered to move to Bootle.

Bucks Park ground then failed to meet Northern Premier League standards, and South dropped out of the league. The club tried to negotiate a ground share with Warrington Town, and also sought planning permission for a ground in the Wavertree sports complex, turned down due to local opposition.

Holly Park was right by the main West Coast railway line into Liverpool Lime Street. Holly Park had been a decent set-up but was in decline when the photos included here were taken. After South Liverpool's departure the ground was flattened and stood empty and derelict for many years. All that remained was the team's name emblazoned on the wall opposite the railway.

Subsequently the new £32m Liverpool South Parkway Station has been built on the site of the old ground as a new interchange for Liverpool Airport.

Photo: Andy Dakin

Photo: Andy Dakin

Horwich RMI F.C.
Grundy Hill

Photo: Andy Dakin

For thirteen years just about the only footballing remnant of Grundy Hill was in the name of the principal shareholders in Hilton Park – the home of Leigh Rugby League team and of Leigh RMI until it also has been sold to become a housing estate.

Horwich Railway Mechanics Institute was the social club based round the major locomotive works at Horwich. The social club itself still exists on Bolton Road, with its large sports field and cricket pitch. The football section was founded in 1896 and made its home on a pitch just a little further up the hill.

The ground developed to the extent that it had a record attendance of 8,500 against Wigan in 1954 in the Lancashire Cup. With seats for 500, there was covered standing on three sides of the pitch.

Above: The Horwich side covered terrace.

However, Grundy Hill's major claim to fame was the corner to corner slope - a 16 foot drop from high to low point on the same pitch. This was so great that it restricted the club's ability to progress up the non-League pyramid.

Consequently the decision was made to relocate the club lock stock and barrel to the rugby town of Leigh. In 1995 Grundy Hill Estates took over ownership of Leigh Centurions` Hilton Park ground, moved the football club in, renamed it Leigh RMI and changed strip as well as name. Meanwhile Grundy Hill became a building site, with the houses of Brooklands and Gresley Avenue on the site of the old ground.

Photo: Colin Peel

Nowadays another Horwich RMI has arisen from the ashes, playing in the Lancashire Amateur League. At the time of writing they were playing their home games in Eccles, but the RMI social club had put in a planning application to create a new ground for them within their Bolton Road complex, just over the Chorley side of the town boundary.

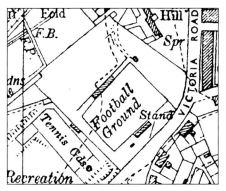

Above: Grundy Hill on a 1955 OS map.

Above: The Horwich side terrace with snow on the Pennines in 1981. Photo: Bob Lilliman
Above, right: The Church Street end terrace showing damage to the roof in 1978, taken from open ground on the the north side.
Photo: Bob Lilliman
Right: The delightful main stand seen in 1978. Photo: Bob Lilliman
Below: A panoramic view from the ground`s highest point. Photo: Colin Peel

Formby F.C.
Brows Lane

There was only one thing wrong with Brows Lane – the club did not own the ground.

Richard Formby, Armour Bearer to King Henry IV, and his descendants became the major landowners of part of the Lancashire coast unsurprisingly known as Formby. The first born male member of each generation had the same first name, and in the latter half of the 20th century Richard Formby was still the major landowner in the area, although living in the Isle of Man. Apparently he progressively sold parcels of land until Brows Lane was the last significant area in his portfolio.

Formby had played at Brows Lane since their formation in 1919, with a record crowd of 2,500 for an FA Cup 1st Round game against Oldham on 24th November, 1973.

Unfortunately their social club and offices were destroyed by fire in September 1990. They were never rebuilt, although they used a portable classroom donated to the club and subsequently taken to Altcar Road (see pages 32/33) when they moved.

At the end of the last century there was a complex situation beyond the scope of this little tome, involving some very well known Merseyside personalities, with the aim of building a new swimming baths complex on Brows Lane.

Below: An aerial view of Brows Lane.
Photo: Mike Floate archive

Photo: Mike Floate

Formby were given a plot of land at Altcar Lane, £175k to build a new stadium on it, and three months notice to vacate the ground. – which was hardly enough time to get it ready to meet the NWCFL grading deadlines. The best summary is probably in the Chairman's Notes in the programme for the last game on their old pitch – "Well, the final match at Brows Lane has finally come around, somewhat quicker than expected due to the unfortunate circumstances the club finds itself in".

Below: The side cover in 2001; an earlier cover is seen below right.
Photo: Mike Floate

Huyton Town F.C., Kirkby Town F.C. & Knowsley United F.C.
Alt Park, Huyton, and Simonswood Lane

This story is complicated, involving multiple club name and ground changes. Alt Park was initially the home of Huyton Rugby League Club, who in season 1985/6 allowed Huyton Town (newly elected to the NWCFL) to ground share with them. This club was believed to be the renamed Prescot BI FC, founder members of the NWCFL who had been kicked out in 1984 as they had installed an artificial pitch. Unfortunately the phoenix only lasted one season, folding in 1986.

Kirkby Town was a long-established club that had played at Simonswood Lane in the Lancashire Combination, the Northern Premier League (between 1970 and 1972), and the Cheshire County League. The club went into liquidation in 1980 due to constant vandalism,

reformed the same year with a new committee, and became founder members of the NWCFL two years later.

The vandals struck again, and they ended that first season ground sharing with Prescot Cables. However, the League would not allow them to continue this arrangement on a longer basis, so they were rejected after just the one season. At that time grants were available for Merseyside, and the club managed to get grant money to restore Simonswood Lane, rejoining the League in 1984.

The club then moved to Alt Park in 1988 and at the same time changed their name to Knowsley United to match the local government reorganisation. The vacant Simonswood Lane was vandalised further, with at least one fire. However, it appears the pitch was still used for Sunday football games into the early 1990's. Subsequently the ground was rebuilt as the magnificent Liverpool FC Academy.

Simonswood Lane. Photo: Andy Dakin

At Alt Park, the new Knowsley United went from strength to strength on the field, gaining promotion to the Northern Premier League in 1991, and reaching the first round of the FA Cup in 1993 when they were defeated at Goodison Park by Carlisle United in front of more than 8,000 fans.

Above: The open terrace on the far side. Photo: Andy Dakin

Despite this crowd, their normal attendances were poor, and new plastic seats they had installed for their run in the qualifying rounds were smashed or burnt over the next few months. The club managed to last until 1997, when they folded once again – but this time finally. Once again, the unused ground was torched and mostly demolished, with some terracing still visible on two sides.

Below & above: The clubhouse end terrace. Photos: Bob Lilliman

Below: The main stand from the clubhouse end terrace. Photo: Bob Lilliman

The main stand and covered terrace at Alt Park. Photo: Bob Lilliman

Curzon Ashton F.C.
National Park

Latterly this was the home of Curzon Ashton FC until 2004. Located between Ashton Police Station and the railway, the ground is now a housing estate.

Above: A packed ground for Ashton National v Hyde Utd. Photo: Tameside Archives .

Originally the ground belonged to the National Gas & Oil Engine Company (hence the ground's name) for their works team Ashton National, playing in the Lancashire Combination. The team reformed after WWII, but not at the same level, and continued playing on the ground until the company closed down.

The ground was derelict for a couple of years before Curzon Ashton renovated it, and played there for a season until Brush Electric took over the old National works and did not allow them to play there. When Brush closed they agreed a lease with Tameside Council.

***Above**: Bob Lilliman's photo from April 1981 shows a small stand on the works side.*

The ground capacity was 5,000 with 350 seats and cover for 450, but Curzon Ashton's record attendance was 1,826 for an FA Vase Semi-Final against Stamford in 1980. At some stage the old stand seen in the Tameside Archive photo had been demolished. A new one was built with the proceeds in1982 from the sale of Steve Wigley to Nottingham Forest.

Above: A covered terrace was built on the site of the old main stand. Photo: Andy Dakin

Newton Heath Loco F.C.
Ceylon Street, Manchester

Look up Newton Heath on Google, and you will find a mixture of football and railway information. Many football sites tell us that Newton Heath Loco was the team that became Manchester United, with only the odd one or two – like the BBC site – having the correct history. They say, "Newton Heath LYR, or *The Heathens*, was the name of Manchester United FC when it was first founded. The LYR stood for Lancashire and Yorkshire Railway, which was added to distinguish them from Newton Heath Loco, who were the Motive Power Division of the company".

At the end of the 19th century Newton Heath had one of the largest railway complexes in the country. There was a carriage works and an enormous locomotive running shed, both within a few hundred yards of each other. The carriage works` team initially played on North Road, on the opposite side of the road to their works, and the loco works played on a pitch on Ceylon Street, just the other side of the tracks from the locomotive sheds. Even in Newton Heath there was a lot of confusion, and many people thought that the original United ground still existed, if unused and overgrown, but the ground they were talking about is the one that used to be Newton Heath Loco.

During the war Newton Heath Loco played in the Manchester League. The 1950 OS map shows the Loco pitch just off Oldham Road in Newton Heath. By that time the ground had two stands, and a considerable amount of terracing. The pitch was fully fenced which made it possible to charge for admittance and so it was often used as the venue for local cup finals and semi-finals. In addition a team called Manchester Northern also used the ground for some time. In the 1960s it was estimated that 260 matches a season were played on Ceylon Street – over 60 being in the last month of the season.

Sadly the press reported that on 27th February, 1970, a fire damaged the 'low tier pavilion and dressing rooms'. Damage was caused to the main stand, dressing rooms, directors` room and storeroom. I can find no record of this ever having been repaired and the ground restored to its previous usage.

The ground was still there in 2006 with the remnants of a covered standing enclosure at the Thorpe Road end, and the foundations of the changing rooms/stand. The covered standing enclosure still had the remains of its roof in the early 1990s, but it was demolished as it provided shelter for the local drug addicts. Since my visit the ground has been turned into yet another housing development.

Below, left: The remains of the Thorpe Road End covered terrace

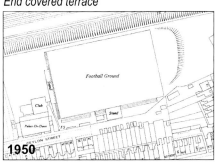

1950

Prestwich Heys A.F.C.
Grimshaws

Photo: Ian Jones

Grimshaws, on Heys Road in Prestwich, was the club's home until 1991. The club was founded in 1938 as the football arm of the Old Boys Association of Heys Road Boys School, and was known as Heys Old Boys AFC until 1964, when they renamed themselves as Prestwich Heys.

Below: Enthusiastic support during Heys 3-1 victory against Finchley in January 1967 - FA Amateur Cup 2nd Round .

In 1967 they won the Lancashire Amateur Cup, and had a proud record in the FA Amateur Cup. As Lancashire Combination Champions they joined the Cheshire County League in 1971, becoming founder members of the NWCFL in which they played for four seasons until 1986 when Grimshaws did not meet the changing ground grading criteria and they moved to the Manchester League.

Photo: Ian Jones

However, Bury Council were anxious to acquire the land as playing fields for Prestwich High School - which had evolved from Heys Road Boys School. With council assistance the club moved to Sandgate Road, which is less than a mile away, in 1991.

Photo: Ian Jones

In the action photos from the 1960`s the railway embankment is now the Metrolink track. The photos also suggest that the pitch was rather sticky on that day. The changing rooms were a wooden building, and the record crowd is thought to be in the region of 3500 during their 1960s cup successes.

The main stand.   Photo: Andy Dakin

Below: Grimshaws, January 1967 with what is now the Metrolink embankment in the distance.

Photo: Ian Jones

Ashton North End F.C.
Manchester Road

Ashton North End joined The Combination in 1894 and were champions in their first season. In 1895 they moved to the Lancashire League, and in 1897 attracted Arthur Wharton – who was the first black professional footballer when playing for Preston North End in 1889 - to join them as captain. In the summer of 1899 they applied to join the Football League, but failed to get a single vote (Middlesbrough being elected). Following this the club was disbanded.

They played at the Athletic Ground on Manchester Road (to the west of Ashton not the north). Being a members club rather than a limited company, the ground did not have turnstiles, which led to interesting differences in attendance figures quoted by the club and the local press. The 1894 OS map shows the ground just off the main Manchester Road.

The site now has the A6140 Moss Way running across the western half of the old pitch, and a factory covering the other half.

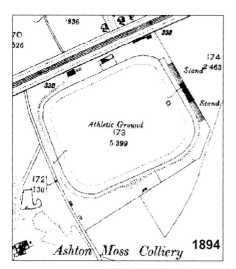

Bootle F.C.
Bucks Park

Bootle FC celebrated its 25th birthday in 1978 at a new stadium on the Northern Perimeter Road. At the same time they changed leagues from the Lancashire Combination to the Cheshire County League, becoming founder members of the NWC.

The 1980's and the new ground saw the club go from strength to strength, and they had some good runs in both the FA Cup and the FA Trophy. The 1980/81 FA Trophy second round saw a Bucks Park record crowd of 750 for a 0-0 draw with Carshalton Athletic.

The land was owned by Bootle Council and with the area becaming a prime site the club were compensated for the lease and relocation promised. The club moved out in 2000, accepting relegation to the NWCFL Second Division as their temporary home – the Kirkby Sports Centre - did not have lights.

Below: A small area of cover by the boardroom in 1993. Below: The end terrace at Bucks Park in 1986. Photos: Rob Lilliman

Bootle F.C. & Bootle Athletic F.C.
Hawthorne Road, Bootle, L20 2DD

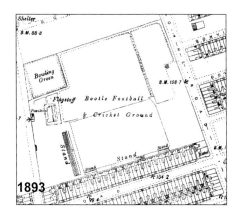

Bootle FC was formed in 1880 as Bootle St Johns by the Deacon of St John's Church, playing on the cricket ground on Hawthorne Road. Their first game in October 1880 was in beating Everton 4-0, crowds of up to 16,000 attended later derbies.

Bootle were not accepted as founder members of the Football League in 1888 but did join the Second Division in 1892. They lasted just one season before resigning due to small crowds and by large travelling expenses.

It is debatable as to when Bootle Athletic was formed and also when they took over the pitch. Many sources quote 1948, but they had played in the Liverpool Leagues before their election to the Lancashire Combination in that year. They folded during the 1953/4 season.

Wadham Road has been built across half of the former football pitch used by both clubs, and the rest of the ground is now the home of Firwood Bootle Cricket Club.

The old pavilion (seen in a photo on the back cover) was used in Football League days and although altered over the years was not demolished until 2002.

Denton F.C.
Ashton Road & Chapel House, Stockport Road

Founder members of The Combination in 1890, Denton were formed several years before that. They saw themselves as aristocrats of the world outside the Football League, objecting to the inclusion of Macclesfield in this new league as they did not believe their football was of an adequate standard. Sadly pride came before the fall, as they won just two games in The Combination's second season, finished last, and dropped out.

After their fall the club reformed and moved to play behind the Chapel House pub on Stockport Road.

They built a superb stand, the opening of which is shown in the Tameside Archive photo below. In 1909/10 they took over the fixtures of Pendlebury in the Lancashire Combination, and continued in that league until WWI. The club did not reform after the war although a Denton club did play in the 1930s.

Heywood United F.C.
Bamford Road

The 1893 OS Map shows Heywood as a hotbed of football, with four grounds clearly marked. One with a clearly marked 'Grand Stand' was on Bamford Road. From the shape of this "Football Field" it looks as though its origins may have been pre-London Association Rules. This was the home of Heywood United, whose origins are lost but who joined the Lancashire Combination in 1902. In the early years of the twentieth century they had average home crowds of 3,000, and in 1913 they paid £800 to sign centre half Andy Browell from Everton. They won the Lancashire Junior Cup in 1914, beating Leyland at Fleetwood – with a special train taking 500 fans.

The club stopped playing soon after the outbreak of WWI and never started again. In the 1960's someone thought of creating a new Heywood United, and was astounded to receive a solicitor's letter saying that the new club would be held responsible for the debts owed by the earlier club of the same name.

The pub built on the site is now demolished, no visible trace of the ground remains, and the area is derelict and plagued by fly tipping.

Maghull F.C.
John Pimbley Recreation Field

On Saturday 11th June, 1927, Lord Vestey, a former Maghull resident, formally declared open the new John Pimbley Recreation Field, complete with its own pavilion. In the picture his wife, Lady Vestey, can be seen addressing the crowd.

Six acres of land in Deyes Lane had been given by John Pimbley of Kensington Farm to create the playing fields, and he also paid most of the £2000 needed to lay out the ground and build the pavilion. After the official opening, the principal guests had tea in the pavilion, and the public had a free tea in a marquee – all courtesy of John Pimbley.

Formed earlier in 1921, Maghull FC quickly made the Recreation Field their home, and they played there until after WWII.

The site of the pavilion is now covered by part of St Andrew's School, and the Recreation Field is a school playing field.

Stantondale F.C.
Orrell Lane L9 8ES

Orrell Lane was the British American Tobacco sports ground, the football team playing in the Liverpool Business Houses League. When the factory closed the team became Stantondale, playing in the Liverpool County Combination. Their success on the pitch led to the team joining the NWCFL in season 1992/3, where they lasted until folding in 1998. However, their last seasons were played at Formby`s Brows Lane.

The pitch was still used after Stantondale left. In a 1998 survey of all playing pitches in the Borough by consultants for Sefton Council, it was reported that the ground was being used by REMYCA in the I Zingari Combination, and by Moss Vale in the Business Houses League. The survey also reported that, "The owner of the site indicated that no football would be played beyond the current season" – and it wasn`t.

The site is still derelict and unused, with only the car park surface remaining within the walls. Plans for development had failed due to the land apparently being unfit to build upon.

Kirkby Sports Centre

An early municipal multi-sport facility (architecture my wife describes as 'Sixties grotty concrete') with a 485 metre cycle track, and the football pitch sat in the middle.

ROMA played here until demolition of the Centre forced them away in 2007. Bootle shared from 2000 until the changing rooms in the Centre were closed in 2002.

Kirkby Sports Centre. Photo: Andy Dakin

Kirkby Sports Centre. Photo: Andy Dakin

Stantondale F.C. Photo: Andy Dakin

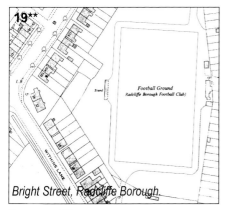

19**

Bright Street, Radcliffe Borough.

Prescot BI
Scotchbarn Lane, Prescot, L34 2TQ

Prescot BI started in 1946 as the works team from the company that had sponsored Prescot Cables prior to WWII, and in 1982 were founder members of the NWCFL. Prescot BI played on the company`s ground on Scotchbarn Lane. Pitch problems led to them installing an Astroturf pitch, but the League did not approve and the club played at Skelmersdale for part of season 1984/5 before they were thrown out in April 1985 and their record expunged. The club continued, playing at Wood Lane in the Liverpool County Combination. The old ground is still in use as a floodlit artifical pitch, but with no stand.

Radcliffe Borough
Bright Street

The club was founded by Jack Pickford on 24th April, 1949, at th`Owd Tower Inn in Sandford Street (still there, but as the dialect dies, now known as "The Old Tower"). Their first few years were spent playing in Ashworth Street, about 400 yards away, in the South East Lancashire League. They soon moved another 300 yards to create a new pitch on land between Bright Street and Bury Road which pre-1950`s OS maps show as open ground. They played there in the Manchester League and then from 1963 in the Lancashire Football Combination. During their time at Bright Street they were able to rail the playing area, build a clubhouse by the Bright Street entrance and a stand on the opposite side of the pitch. However, it doesn't appear that they ever got the ground to the standard necessary for entry into the FA Cup or the FA Trophy.

Unfortunately the land was privately owned, and in 1970 the club had to leave to make way for housing development, and now Wilton Gardens covers the area. They found a new patch of land at Stainton Park, managed to negotiate out of covenants forbidding the sale of alcohol on the land, and moved in.

Prescot BI. Photo: Andy Dakin.

Index

Photo: Liverpool Weekly News / South Liverpool programme cover 1969/70